The Fall and Redemption of Man

Selected, arranged and rendered
into Modern English from the Chester,
Coventry, Lincoln, Norwich, Wakefield
and York Mystery Plays

John Bowen

ALRA
www.alra.co.uk

Samuel French – London
New York – Sydney – Toronto – Hollywood

THE FALL AND REDEMPTION OF MAN

First performed on 5th December 1967, at the LAMDA Theatre, Logan Place, London, W8, by students at the beginning of their second year, with the following cast:

God; 1st King; 1st Shepherd; Man with a Pot; Knight at Pilate's Court; Simon of Cyrene	Thomas Cloney
Adam; 2nd King; 2nd Shepherd; Philip; Annas	Colin Baker
Gabriel; 3rd Woman with Child; 2nd Woman of Jerusalem; Veronica	Patricia Ludwick
2nd Angel; Neighbour; Mak; 1st Knight Massacring Innocents; John; Pilate	David Saxon
Eve; Neighbour; Sheep; 2nd Woman with Child; Doctor; 1st Woman of Jerusalem	Dorothy Baddeley
Satan	Aidan Murphy
3rd King; 3rd Shepherd; Knight-Torturer	Raymond Lee
Tree; the Virgin Mary; Hysterical Woman During Scourging	Celia Quicke
Cain; Herald; James; Caiphas	David Peart
Abel; Ass; 2nd Knight Massacring Innocents; Jesus Christ; Porter	Paul Taylor
Greenhorn; Elizabeth; Gil; 1st Woman with Child; Magdalene; an Angel	Rowan Wiley
Joseph; Judas; Herod Agrippa; Torturer's Assistant	James MacInnes
Citizen on Urgent Business; Herod; Peter	Eran Banael
2nd Knight at Pilate's Court	

Lighting: Brian Benn

Stage Manager: Stuart Munro

D S M: Jennifer Lordon

SETTING

A large and solid platform represents the pageant. Under it there are stools for the actors to sit on, and all their props are there. Upon it and at the back of it are two much smaller platforms representing the towers. The platform I have in mind as I write is 16 feet wide, 12 feet deep, and 5 feet high. The tower at SL, which is the tower that will represent Heaven and Calvary, is 2 feet high, that at SL is 1 feet, 6 inch high. Both are 4 feet by 4 feet. Steps lead from them to the level of the pageant platform.

Two flights of steps lead from the top of the pageant to ground level—or stage level if this production should be presented on a conventional stage. One, at extreme SR runs from the front of the pageant downstage, making a right angle with it. The other, at SL, runs sideways, so that its length extends the width of the pageant. Full-length mirrors are set at each side of the pageant.

Before the performance begins, all props for Act I are set beneath the pageant, by the places of the actors who will use them. The tree of knowledge—a stylized structure to which a few apples have been tied (the string goes right through the apple)—has been set on the pageant between the two towers.

For
BRIAN and DOROTHY PHELAN,
JOSHUA
and KATE

INTRODUCTION

This is a play for acting: it is not for those whose first consideration is a serious study of the texts of the Mystery Plays. Serious students of the texts may be either vexed or amused at the way I have taken so many lines from here, so many from there, dodging in one scene all about the northern counties, have run the two Wakefield Shepherds' Plays together, have cut and reshaped, and have left out the Resurrection altogether. But for students of the texts, there are the texts themselves, and the adaptations of the Chester Plays by Mr Maurice Hussey, the Wakefield Plays by Mr Martial Rose and the York Plays by the Rev. Dr J. S. Purvis. This play was constructed as an acting exercise for students of the London Academy of Dramatic Art to perform publicly in their own theatre. The criteria that governed my making of it were, first that it should work as a play before an audience, secondly that it should provide parts of approximately equal length and importance for the twelve students who were to perform it, and last that the students should learn something of themselves and something of acting by doing it.

As to whether the play works in the theatre, I will say only that it seemed to do so when the students performed it, that it was praised by, among others, Mr Harold Hobson of the *Sunday Times* and Mr B. A. Young of the *Financial Times*, and that Mr Young told his readers that he had been moved to tears by the end of it. I can say something about the staging. LAMDA is fortunate in having an excellent small theatre which can be adapted to most kinds of performance, from the use of a proscenium arch to theatre in the round. I used, as readers of the text will see, a kind of stylized pageant wagon and an area in front of it which might be considered as the street. The back of the theatre was hung with black drapes (a good sky cloth could as well be used, but will present problems in lighting out shadows), so I had my pageant painted in circus colours of red and gold to keep all cheerful. Acting on the pageant was necessarily "out front" and needed a fair amount of projection, since the performers were five feet in the air. The movable seat-blocks of the theatre were arranged in a semicircle (a little less than semi in fact) so that acting in the street was "in the round" acting, close to the audience. Clearly this way of staging can be adapted to open-stage, and to a proscenium arch if the stage is deep enough, but I don't think it can be adapted completely to theatre-in-the-round because there is then nowhere to place the pageant.

Next, the parts. I was given half the second-year students at LAMDA in December 1967 as a cast: there were eight men and four women. The clear intention of the play is that what the audience sees is "A group of young actors presenting a Mystery Play": there must be doubling, trebling and quadrupling of parts, and the audience sees the actors become each separate character, usually by putting on or bringing on some easily identifiable article of clothing or a property—Pilate, for instance, comes down the steps, goes into the pageant, R, takes off his toga, comes straight out again, L, puts on his halo before the mirror, and enters at once as a Disciple. The audience, in my own experience, is never confused, accepts each character as a separate being, and is capable of being very much moved when a young actress in white polo-neck sweater and black skirt with a blue headscarf mourns the death of her son, although they have seen the same actress a few minutes before, in the same costume, but with a black scarf, mocking Jesus with a crown of thorns, and crying, "Roll up for the king" (an improvised line). However, twelve is not a magic number: the play cannot be done with fewer actors, but it can be done with more. And, even if one stayed with twelve, nine men and three women, would be better than eight and four—I had to use an actress for the Doctor in Act II: she played him very well, like the principal of a ladies' college in a beard.

Lastly, what is learned. The audience (I think) learns something, or at least is reminded of what it may often forget, which is that to those who wrote, and acted in, and watched the Mystery Plays, what was being played was not a symbolic statement of a religious truth, but history. So much attention tends to be paid to "the play as ritual" that we forget that here were people who saw God as a King-in-Parliament, Lucifer as a rebellious Duke, Joseph as an old man past potency who had been dragooned into marrying a young ward of the temple, Cain as a struggling farmer, and who knew that the women who mourned Christ on the cross *did not know* that the Resurrection was to follow, so that surprise and anger were mixed up with their grief. This play, as I have arranged it from a great wealth of material, makes a shape in which the first part ends with an execution and a mourning parent, and so does the second, and it is concerned as much with human as with religious matters, though the story it tells is what the title says it is.

However, what do the actors learn? First, as I have said, they experience both "out front" and "in the round" acting in the same play, and must modify and extend their technique to comprehend both. More importantly, at a time when more and more attention is being given in schools to what is called "contact acting"—that is, the necessary and important process of *working with* other actors, getting and giving to create something shared, a situation or a scene, something which is worked out in action together— sometimes too little attention is given to another aspect of acting which is also necessary and important, and which is *contact with the audience*. "Contact acting", when it is bad, can be very private: a group of contact actors can make together what is a truthful statement about the nature of life, and then decide that they would only compromise the statement if they were to take pains to present it to an audience.

Well, if you are acting in the open on top of a wagon, to a restless audience which has not paid to see you, you have to take such pains, and by reminding my cast of the pageant and the street (and stationing a "crowd" of twenty-four first-year students in the front row) I was able to exercise them in this necessary craft, and they were all the more exercised in that, if one is playing four or five different parts in the course of one evening, one is forced to make an immediate contact with the audience, if only to say, "Now I'm an ass. Now I'm Caiphas." And of course, to play such a variety of parts, and play them clearly, the students were forced away from what is another vice of mid-twentieth-century acting, the "I can't do anything ham or untruthful, by which I mean anything in the least unlike myself" kind of acting, and discovered that to begin with the exterior of characterization is often a valid way to the inside.

This begins to sound as if I were riding a hobby-horse. I don't mean to do so. It remains for me to thank Mr Norman Ayrton, the Principal of LAMDA, for allowing me to conduct this experiment in teaching and directing, and also to thank the highly talented group of second-year students who performed the play. The editions of the texts I used in making my own selection and adaptation of material are listed below:

Sources

York Plays. The plays performed by the Crafts of Mysteries of York on the day of Corpus Christi. Ed. Lucy Toulmin Smith (Oxford, 1885).

Early English Text Society:

Extra Series LXII, The Chester Plays, Part I. Ed. Dr Hermen Deimling (London, 1893).

Extra Series CXV, The Chester Plays, Part II. Ed. Dr Matthews (London, 1916).

Extra Series LXXXVII, Two Coventry Corpus Christi Plays. Ed. Hardin Craig (London, 1902).

Extra Series CXX, Ludus Coventriae or The Plaie Called Corpus Christi. Ed. K. S. Block (London, 1922).

Extra Series LXXO, The Towneley Plays. Ed. George England (London, 1897).

Extra Series CIV, The Non-Cycle Mystery Plays together with the Croxton Play of the Sacrament and "The Pride of Life". Ed. Osborn Waterhouse (London, 1909).

ACT I

The house lights are up. The actors enter in ones and twos. All wear white polo-neck sweaters. The girls wear black skirts over black tights. The men wear black trousers

They greet the friends they may see in the audience, and then take their places beneath the pageant. They check their props. Since each actor will take many parts, they will not be identified in this script except by the part taken at the time. When the actors are seated and have checked their props, the house lights are lowered and the pageant area is lit

God leaves his place beneath the pageant, bringing with him a mitre and crook. He leaves the pageant by the side, L—none of the actors will ever enter or leave their own space beneath the pageant by the front, though either side may be used

God puts his mitre on and adjusts it, then climbs the steps L, and goes on up to the tower. He faces the audience, and speaks to them

God   My name is known: God and King.
I am most in majesty.
In whom no beginning may be
And no end. Highest in potency
I am, and have been ever.

I have made stars and planets in their courses to go.
I have made a moon for the night
And a sun to light the day also.
I have made earth where trees and grasses spring.
Beasts and fowl, both great and small,
Fishes in the teeming sea, all
Thrive and have my liking.
I have made all of nothing for man's sustenation,
And of this pleasant garden that I have most goodly planted
I will make him gardener for his recreation.
(*Calling*) Now come forth, Adam, to Paradise.

Adam leaves his place and comes up the stairs L. He is followed by Gabriel and another Angel, who present Adam before God's tower

Thou shalt have all manner of things,
Both flesh and foul, and fruit of price.
Here is hot spices and sweet liquorice.
Take them all at thy liking,
Apple and pear, and gentle rice.

> In eating thou shalt eat of every growing tree,
> Except the tree of knowledge, which I forbid thee.
> For in what day soever thou eatest *there*, thou shalt be
> Even as the child of death. Take heed.
> And thus I say,
> It is not good for man alone to be.
> Therefore I make thee a helper to comfort thee.
> And first I cause a sleep to come on thee.

Adam sleeps on the steps of the tower R. *God mimes the removal of a rib, without actually touching Adam. The mime is co-operative, Adam being affected by the removal, though as if still sleeping*

> In sleep thou art now, well I see.
> Therefore a rib I take of thee,
> And flesh also, to make a wife for thee.

God gives the imaginary rib to the Angel who puts it on the downstage steps of the rostrum, R. *Then he goes to the top of the steps,* R. *Eve has come out of the pageant,* R. *The Angel moves his arms as though pulling her by invisible strings. She climbs to the top of the pageant and goes to sleep near Adam*

> Adam, awake, arise!
> And take Eve unto thee, that you both be as one
> To comfort one another when I am gone.

Adam and Eve wake slowly. They wonder at each other. They touch one another, without sensuality, as children touch a new object to try to understand it

Meanwhile, Satan leaves the pageant, L. *He puts on a black half-mask with curving horns, admiring himself in the mirror. He comes up the steps* L *stopping before he reaches the top, so that he can eavesdrop, hidden*

Adam   Oh, bone of my bones, and flesh of my flesh,
         Thou shalt be called Woman, because thou art of me.
Eve   Oh, gift of God most goodly, to have made us so like!
         Most sweet Adam, I do much rejoice of thee.
Adam   Therefore God be praised, such comfort to give,
         That each with the other so pleasantly may live.

Angel indicates God. They rise and stand before him

> Oh, Lord, most mickle is thy might
> That here is shown on every side.
> For now here is a joyful sight
> To see this world, so long and wide.
Eve   Many diverse things there are,
         Of beasts and fowls, both wild and tame.
         But none is made to thy likeness
         But we alone. Loved be thy name!
Adam   Oh, blessed Lord, now at thy will

	Since we are wrought, vouchsafe to tell, What shall we do, and where to dwell?
God	For this skill I made you this day My name to worship everywhere. You shall love me and praise me now and always. For my making I ask no more. Now, Adam, go forth and be prince in place. But as I said before when thou wert alone, In eating thou mayst eat of every tree there is But of the tree of knowledge of good and evil, Lest thou die the death by doing so amiss. I will depart now where my habitation is.

Both God and Gabriel turn their backs on the action. Angel remains to watch

Adam	Holy Father, blessed be thou, For I may walk in wealth enow. All this creation is servant to me; I have no need to touch the tree. I am a good gardener: Every fruit I may garner here.
Eve	We may be both blithe and glad Our Lord's commandment to fulfil. Every tree with fruit is spread. Our wits were wilful, and our deeds bad To work against our good Lord's will.
Adam	In his garden let us go see All the flowers of fair beauty And taste the fruits of great plenty That be in Paradise.

Angel, standing by Eve, mimes a butterfly with his hands. Eve gives a little cry of delight and pleasure and runs after it. Angel releases it to her. She shows it to Adam. He takes it from her, and sits on the steps of the tower, R, to examine it more closely. She puts her hands on his shoulder, then wanders a little away to pick a flower. She plaits imaginary flowers into her hair. While:

Satan	Now, now of my purpose I doubt not to attain. I cannot abide that in this joy they shall be. No. I will tempt them to sin into their pain By subtlety to catch them, the way I clearly see. (*He approaches Eve*)

Angel crosses to protect her with his cloak, but Satan pushes his arm away

	Hail, fair wife and comely dame!
Eve	Who is there?
Satan	I, that a friend am. I come for thy good. For tell me: why was God so nice To order so, against thy delight,

	That of all trees of Paradise
	You should forsake the meat?
Eve	No, of the fruit of every tree,
	To eat good leave have we.
Satan	Every tree?
Eve	Save of the fruit of one, we must flee.
	That tree that in the middle is.
	If we eat of it, we do amiss.
	And God said we should die.

Satan (*laughing*) Die?

Eve	If we but touch that tree.
Satan	God is cunning, and wise of wit,
	And knows well, if you should eat of it,
	Then your eyes should be unknit.
	Like gods, you should be.
Eve	Gods?
Satan	Yes, and know good and evil also.
	It was therefore he bade you forfend.
	You may well see he was your foe.
	As I am your friend.

(*He indicates the tree, but does not touch the fruit*)

	Taste of his fruit, and try it.
	It is good meat: I avow it.
	And if it be not to your quiet,
	Say that I am false.
Eve	Ah, lord this tree is fair and bright,
	Green and seemly in my sight,
	The fruit sweet and full of might,
	If it will make us gods.

(*She takes an apple off the tree; holds it, afraid to bite*)

Satan	Bite on boldly. Be nought abashed,
	And bear one to Adam to make him happy.
	You shall be like gods, most certainly.
	That I speak true, soon shalt thou see.

(*He retires to his eavesdropping position, cocking a snook at
    God's back as he goes*)

Eve	Wait!

*She tries to follow him, but he is gone. Hesitantly, she returns to the tree. Then
she takes another apple off the tree, and goes to Adam*

	Adam, husband, life and dear,
	Eat some of this apple here,
	As wise as God is, we may be,
	And we shall be God's peer.
Adam	Alas, woman, why took thou this?
	God gave commandment to us both
	We should forfend this tree of his.
	Thy work will make him wrath.

Eve	Nay, Adam, grieve not at it,
	And I shall say the reason why.
	We shall be as gods, you and I.
	All God's wisdom to understand.
	We shall make fish and flesh, sea and sand,
	Birds and sweet water and land.
	Take thou this apple from my hand,
	And taste it.

Angel tries ineffectually to stop them

Adam (*tempted*)	To eat it would I not eschew,
	If I were sure thou spake the truth.
Eve	Bite on boldly, for it is true.
	We shall be gods in very sooth.
Adam	To win that name,
	I shall taste it at thy teaching.

Adam and Eve hold up the apples, hesitate for the last time, then bite together. Adam cries out

Angel returns to the rostrum, R

	Alas! What have I done? For shame!
	Ah, Eve, thou art to blame.
	To this thou hast enticed me.
	For I am naked, as I think.
	(*He covers his members*)
Eve	Alas! And so am I!
	(*She covers herself also*)
Adam	Now for sad sorrow we must sink,
	Since we have grieved God Almighty
	That made me man,
	Broken his bidding bitterly.
	Alas, that ever it began!
	This work, Eve, hast thou wrought,
	And made this bad bargain.

An actor leaves the pageant, R, and comes briskly up the steps. He carries two fig leaves. When he gets to the tower, R, he becomes a Tree, with a fig leaf at the end of each branch

Eve	Adam, husband, let us take
	These fig-leaves for shame's sake.
	And for our members a hiding make
	Of them for thee and me.

Both Adam and Eve pick the leaves and try to cover themselves

Adam	Therewith my members I will hide.
	And under this tree I will abide.
	For if by the Lord God we be spied,
	Out of this place go we.

God and the two Angels turn

God   Adam!

Adam and Eve cling close together. Tree's branches droop

                 Adam!

Adam and Eve look at each other. Eve nudges Adam. Tree quivers

Adam   Lord?
God   Adam, where art thou?

Tree puts down its branches, and pushes them out of its shelter. They cannot see God

Adam   I hear thee, Lord, but see thee not.
God   What dost thou do, what hast thou wrought?
Adam   We are naked, and therefore hide.
God   Who told thee, Adam, thou naked was,
                 Save only thine own trespass?
                 Thou hast eaten of the tree
                 That I forbade thee.

Adam pushes Eve in front of him. She resists and pushes him in front of her. Then he her again. While:

Adam   Lord, this woman that is here,
                 That thou gavest me to my wife,
                 She tempted me, and at her prayer,
                 I ate of the tree of life.
God   Unwise woman, tell me why
                 Thou hast done this foul folly.
                 I made thee a great lady
                 In Paradise to live joyfully.
Eve   Lord, when thou wentest from this place
                 A serpent with an angel's face
                 Promised we should be full of grace
                 If we did eat, both twain.
                 I did his bidding. Alas, alas!
                 Now we be bound in death to pass.
                 I suppose it was Satan as
                 Has put us to this pain.

God turns to Satan, who comes up to the platform from the steps

God   Why didst thou, Serpent, in this wise
                 Prevent my grace?
Satan   I shall tell thee wherefore and why
                 I did all this felony.
                 For I am full of great envy
                 Of wrath and wicked hate,
                 That man should live above the sky

Where at one time dwelled I,
Who now am cast into hell's sty
Straight out at Heaven's gate.
God   Cursed art thou, that my commandment didst defile,
Above all cattle and beasts. For this woman's sake,
Upon thy belly thou shalt go
And eat the earth, to and fro,
And enmity between you two,
Henceforth will I make.
(*He raises his hand*)

Satan feels himself slowly pressed down to the earth, but manages to remain on his back. God's hand describes a flipping-over gesture. Satan does a backward somersault, and is on his belly. He hisses at God, and slithers away down the steps. God turns to Adam and Eve. Angel motions to them to kneel

Thou, woman, thou shalt bring forth children with pain,
And be subject to thy husband. And thy lust shall pertain
To him. I have determined this ever to remain.
And to thee, man, for that my voice thou didst abstain
Cursed be the earth for ever for thy sake.
Thy living shalt thou get with sweat and pain
Till thou shalt return to dust, whereof I did thee make.
Thou hast been as one of us, good and evil to know.
Therefore I shall exclude thee from this place,
Lest of the tree of life thou shouldst eat and grow.
So, Cherubim, my angels bright,
To middle-earth, go drive these two.
Gabriel   All ready, Lord, as it is right,
Since thy will is it be so,
And thy liking.
Adam and Eve, now do you go,
For here you may make no dwelling.

Angel stands Adam and Eve up. He points to the steps, R. Adam and Eve move to them. Tree insists on having its leaves back. Gabriel stands guard at the top of the steps, L, Angel at R. Lights up on the ground area as Adam and Eve descend to it

Angel   Go ye forth, fast to fare.
Of sorrow may ye sing.

Adam and Eve reach the bottom of the steps, and look about them miserably

Eve   Alas, alas and well-a-day
That ever I did touch the tree!
In black bushes my bower shall be.
My husband is hurt because of me.
Now stumble we on stalk and stone.
My wit away from me is gone.
Husband, turn thy hand to me,

	And twist my neck from my neck bone.

Adam   Woman, wife, turn from this thought.
Thy wit, it is not worth a rush.
I will not slay flesh of my flesh,
For of my flesh, thy flesh was wrought.
And if that I should slay my wife,
I slay myself with that same knife,
In Hell's dark dale to lead my life.
No, let us walk forth unto the land,
With labour and dolour our food to find,
Delving and digging with my hand.
And, wife, to spin now you must try,
Our naked bodies in cloth to wind,
Till God shall some small comfort send
With grace to relieve our careworn minds.

Eve   Alas that ever we wrought this sin
Our bodily sustenance for to win!
Now you shall delve, and I shall spin,
In care to lead our lives.

*Adam is about to step off, but Eve reaches out a hand to detain him. He turns.
They look at each other, Eve frankly longing. A moment. She draws him
closer, then suddenly holds him. An embrace. Then she draws him down. They
lie together. They are no longer at all like children*

Satan draws himself up, using the steps, to watch

Adam and Eve roll over and over

*Cain and Abel come from the pageant, R, beside the steps. First Cain, then
Abel kneels by the side of their parents. Adam and Eve are still. Then they rise.
Each takes a child's hand. Then they draw Cain and Abel to their feet. The
children are now grown. Adam and Eve lead them off a little way, then Adam
turns to them*

Adam   Cain and Abel, my children dear,
Now I make you know in good manner;
You were the first-fruits of human engender,
For your mother and I were never of man's nature,
But of another portraiture.
Wherefore I counsel you in good advice,
You should offer to God in sacrifice
Your own first-fruits of all he sends.

Abel   Thank you, father, for your good doctrine.
As you have taught us, so shall we do.
And as for me, through God's grace divine,
I will forthwith apply me thereto.

Cain   And though I am loth, so will I also.

Adam   Then, Cain, you shall be a husbandman,
And Abel a shepherd be.

	Cain, offer corn both fresh and clean
	To God in majesty.
	And, Abel, while thy life shall last.
	Thou shalt offer thy first-born beast.
Cain	To thy counsel, father, I incline,
	But I'd just as well go home to dine.

Adam and Eve hesitate, worried at this surliness, then go off into the pageant, L

Greenhorn, a horse, comes out of the pageant, R, *and gets into position for Cain to plough*

Abel puts a brotherly arm on Cain's shoulder. It is shrugged off. Abel goes off to the pageant R *and picks up a toy lamb from among his props. Meanwhile, Cain begins to mime ploughing*

Cain (*to his mare*) Hup! Hup. Greenhorn! Hup, you devil!
Draw on! Oh, God give you evil.
What? . . . Will you go no farther, mare?
You shrew. Pull on! Pull on! Go fare!
God give you sorrow and care!
Lo! Lo! Down now!
Before God thou art the worst mare
That ever I had in plough.

Abel returns, carrying his lamb

Abel	God speed you, brother.
Cain	Kiss my arse!
Abel	Dear brother, as you know——
Cain	Go grease thy sheep!
Abel	No, brother, we must both go
	To worship God, and pay him our fee,
	Corn or cattle, whatever it be.
Cain	Oh, let out your geese: the fox will preach.
	Should I leave my plough, and everything,
	And go with thee to make offering?

Greenhorn indicates that he should

	No, I am not so mad.
	Go to the devil, and say I bade thee.
	What does God give thee to praise him so?
	To me he gives nothing but sorrow and woe.
Abel	Cain, leave this vain carping.
	For God gives thee all thy living
	Come, let us be walking.
	I wish our tithe were proffered.
Cain	Why should I tithe, brother?
	Each year I'm more poor than the other.
Abel	Yet all the good thou hast won
	Comes from God's grace alone.

Cain	Nay, God has always been my foe.
Abel	Dear brother, say not so.
	But let us forth together go.
Cain	Oy-yo-yoy! Whither so fast?

The devil speed me if I haste.
As long as I hold my living,
To God or man
I'll make no haste in giving
Of what I've won.
What need have I my work to lose
To wear out my shoes and tear my hose?
Go you to tithe before me.

Abel   That would give our father anxiety.
We must go together.
For are you not my brother?

Cain   Well, then, I see
That go I must, willy nilly.
Bide thou there, Greenhorn.

Cain leads Greenhorn to the left and goes into the pageant

Abel comforts Greenhorn. Cain returns with token sheaves. Greenhorn lashes out at him. He kicks her rump and she goes on into the pageant

Now wend we our way.

They go together to the foot of the steps, R

Lay down thy bundle upon this hill.

Abel   Forsooth, brother, so I will.
(He puts the lamb well up on the steps)

Cain   Thou shalt tithe first, an' if thou would.

Abel   God that made both Heaven and earth,
I pray thee now to hear my plea,
And take in thanks, if it be worth,
This tithe I offer here to thee.
For I give it in good intent
To thee, My Lord, that has all sent.

Abel mimes striking flint, getting a spark, and putting smouldering tinder to the wood. He and Cain fall back as if flames had shot up. The Angel picks up the lamb

Cain   Now, if thou hast done, let me
Offer my tithe to his divinity.
(He mimes sorting out sheaves from his sack. But whatever it may have been his first intention to give, it becomes harder and harder for him to give anything, so that he hesitates, thinks better, and puts sheaf after sheaf to one side for himself)
One. And one. And that makes two.
But neither of these sheaves I will forgo.

Two. And this one. That makes three.
But that also shall stay with me.
(*Mumbling*)
Mmmmm. Nnnnerr. Four. But look you here
I grew no better corn this year.
Thistles and briars I got great plenty,
And all kinds of weeds, as many as might be.
Four. Five. Six. And this makes seven.
But you'll not get this neither, God in Heaven.
Nor yet the next four, in my might
Shall never come within God's sight.
Now number next.
(*Cheerfully*) *This* we may miss.

Abel   Cain, thou tithest wrong, and of thy worst.
Methinks of God thou hast no dread.

Cain   If he get more, the devil me speed.
One sheaf's his bargain. No more great nor small
As he may wipe his arse withal.
For that sheaf, and all that lies here
Have cost me full dear.
Before it was cut and brought to stack,
I had many a weary back.

Abel   Cain, tithe rightly, and in good kind.

Cain   As for how I'm tithing, never you mind.
You tend your scabby sheep, and shut your gob.
Twelve. Thirteen—ah, just the job.
God can have this one; and that makes two.
And for my soul, that's as far as I'll go.
(*Laying imaginary sticks*)
But since you've tithed and tendered thine,
Now will I set fire unto mine.
(*He sets imaginary flint to steel, lights his imaginary tinder, and sets it to the imaginary wood. There is no fire. Only smoke*)
Puff! Puff! Haw! Help me to blow.
It will not burn for me, I trow.

Abel does so. Both fall back, coughing

This smoke does me much shame.
Now burn in the devil's name!

Abel   Cain, this is not worth a leek.
Thy tithe should burn without smoke.

Cain   Oh, kiss the devil right in the arse.
Let it burn the way it does.

Gabriel turns, and moves C

Gabriel   Cain, do not so rebel
Against thy brother, Abel.

>Thou shouldst neither swear nor chide.
>If thou tithest right, thou getst thy mede.

Gabriel turns back. Cain is confounded

Cain   Now who was that hob-over-the-wall?
               Eh? Who was that who piped so small?
               God must be out of his wits.
               Come on, Abel, let us wend.
               Methinks God is not my friend.
               So I will do a flit.
               (*He moves away*)

Abel picks up the sheaf from the steps and follows

Abel   Oh, brother, that was ill done.
Cain   Well, if it was, let it alone,
               And we will move on.
               For if I may, I would be
               Where God can no longer see me.
Abel   No, dear brother, I must fare
               To the field where our beasts are.
Cain   No, not you. We're still disputing.
               And now's the time to make a quitting.
Abel   Brother, why art thou so in ire?
Cain   Why did thy tithe take the fire
               When mine but smoked
               So we were like to have choked?
Abel   God's will, I think it were,
               That mine burned so clear.
Cain   Ah! Was it?
               (*He stoops and picks up an imaginary weapon*)
               Then let you pay for it.
               For with this cheekbone
               I shall strike you down.

Cain strikes. Abel falls. The sheaf falls to the ground

               So lie down there, and take your rest.
               Thus shall shrews be chastised best.
Abel   Vengeance, vengeance, Lord, I cry,
               For I am slain, and not guilty.
Cain   Yoh! Lie there, old shrew! Lie there! Lie!

Abel dies. Cain turns to the audience

               And if any of you think I did amiss,
               I will make it worse than it is.
               (*He returns to the body, striking it savagely*)

God steps from his tower to the front of the pageant. The Angels go back into the background

God   Cain! Cain!

Cain hastily gets between God and Abel's body, to hide it

Cain   Who is that who calls me?
                 (*He points away*)
                 I am yonder. Can you not see?
God   Cain, where is thy brother, Abel?
Cain   My brother's keeper who made me?
                 I cannot tell where he may be.
                 Perhaps he is sleeping.
God   What hast thou done, thou wicked man?
                 Thy brother's blood cries out on thee.
Cain   He is not in my keeping.
God   For the deed thou has done this day
                 Cursed on earth thou shalt be aye.
                 Thou shalt be cursed on the ground,
                 Unprofitable where so'eer thou wend.
                 And to whatever work thou turnst thy hand
                 It shall be vain, and naught, and nothing sound.

Pause. Then Cain defies God

Cain   Well, deal out thy curses, for I will have none,
                 Nor take such from thee when I am gone.
                 For since I have done such a great sin
                 That I may not thy mercy win,
                 And thou dost bar me from thy grace,
                 I will hide me from thy face.
                 And where I am found by any man,
                 Let him slay me, if he can.
                 In the street, or in the sty,
                 Let him try as I pass by.
                 And bury me with a joyful heart
                 Since for all men, I do not give a fart.

*Cain has his back to all three sides of the audience and is able to slip a liquid
blood capsule into his mouth during God's speech*

God   Nay, Cain, thou shalt not die soon,
                 Horribly though thou has done.
                 It is not thy fellows' boon
                 Thy blood for to shed.
                 But forsooth who slayeth thee
                 Sevenfold shall punished be.
                 Thy great penance thou mayest not flee
                 For thy wicked deed.
                 Therefore a token shalt thou see.
                 It shall be printed so on thee
                 That every man shall know full well
                 Thou art Cain did his brother kill.

Cain gives a loud cry and bites on the blood capsule

God retires

Cain turns back to Abel's body. The actor's face must become animal-like, with blood dripping from the corner of the mouth

The Lights fade on the pageant

Satan leaves his watching position and crawls on his belly towards Cain

The Lights fade on all but the area round the body

Satan reaches Cain. He picks up the sheaf that Abel dropped. He uses Cain's own body as a prop to pull himself slowly upright. Then he stands, proudly, without help, holding up the sheaf in one hand, resting on Cain's head or shoulder, while Cain lours brutishly at the audience

The Lights on the body area fade to a Black-out

All actors, except God and Gabriel return to the pageant

Two Angels enter

The Lights come up on the top of the pageant

God   For the wretchedness of the needy
                 And the poor's lamentation,
                 Now shall I respond that am God Almighty.
                 The time has come for reconciliation.
                 My prophets with prayers have made supplication.
                 My contrite creatures all for comfort cry.
                 All my angels in Heaven without cessation
                 Beseech me grant to man both grace and mercy.
                 Therefore from us, God, thou, Angel Gabriel, shall we send
                 Into the country of Galilee.
                 There to the town of Nazareth thou shalt wend,
                 And find a maiden—though wedded to a man is she:
                 Joseph his name, of the house of David.
                 For thus I have the fiend beguiled
                 To cause this maiden to be wed.
                 From forth her virgin womb shall come a child
                 Who will get for men more grace than ever they had.
                 Her maidenhead by no man shall be defiled.
                 She shall bear the son of Almighty God.
                 And for Adam, that now lies in sorrow's bane,
                 This glorious birth shall redeem him again
                 From bondage and thrall.
                 This deed shall be done in Israel, before my throne,
                 And shall delight you all.

God and the two Angels return to the pageant, using the steps L

Mary leaves the pageant R *and comes half-way up the steps. Gabriel adances to meet her. Lights come up on the lower area*

Gabriel	Hail, Mary, full of grace!
	Our Lord God is with thee.
	Above all women what ever was.
	Lady, blessed thou shalt be.
Mary (*frightened*)	Almighty Father, King of Bliss,
	From all delusions save me now!
	Invisibly my spirit troubled is.
	I am amazed, and know not what to do.

Gabriel takes her hand and brings her up the steps

Gabriel	Dread thee nothing, maid, of this.
	From Heaven above, hither am I sent,
	An embassage from that very King of Bliss
	Unto thee, lady and virgin reverent,
	Saluting thee here as most excellent,
	Whose virtue above all others' doth abound.
	For in thee shall grace be found,
	And thou shalt conceive upon this ground
	The Second Person of God Enthroned.
	He shall be born of thee alone.
	Without sin thou shalt him conceive.
	Thy grace and thy goodness will never be gone,
	But in virginity thou shalt ever live.
Mary	I marvel much how that may be.
	I never yet knew any man's company.
Gabriel	The Holy Ghost shall light on thee.
	The child that shall of thee be born
	Is the Second Person of the Trinity.
	He shall save those that were forlorn
	And destroy the fiend's power utterly.

Elizabeth comes from the pageant, R and walks round to the front. She has a pillow strapped to her belly. Lights come up on the ground area

> Discomfort thee not, Mary.
> For to God, nothing impossible may be.
> See now, thy cousin, Elizabeth—.
> Elizabeth, that barren was——

Elizabeth puts a hand to her belly and gives a cry of joy. Two actors hurry from the pageant, R, to her. She mimes her delight and surprise, showing them her condition

> As thou mayst see, conceived has
> In age a son, through God's grace.
> And now with child she has been
> Six months and more, as shall be seen.

Mary	Then with all meekness I incline to his accord,
	Bowing down my head with all benignity.
	See here the handmaiden of our great Lord.
	After his will, may all be done to me.

Mary kneels in front of Gabriel who wraps his cloak over her bowed head and shoulders

Gabriel   Now blessed be the time set
      When thou wast born in thy degree.
      For now is the knot surely knit,
      And God conceived in Trinity.
      (*He unfolds his cloak and retires*)

Mary looks after him wonderingly. Then she turns, and runs joyfully down to meet Elizabeth. They embrace. Neighbours retire a little distance

Mary   Elizabeth, my own cousin,
      I do desire of all the most
      To speak with thee of all my kin.
      Therefore I come thus in this haste.
Elizabeth Welcome, mild Mary,
      My own cousin so dear.
      A joyful woman am I,
      Now I see thee here.
      When thou didst greet me, sweet Mary,
      The child stirred in my body,
      For great joy of thy company
      And the fruit that is in thee.
Mary   Elizabeth, now will I
      Thank the Lord, king of mercy
      With joyful mirth and melody,
      And praise him to his liking.
      "Magnificat" while I can,
      "Anima mea dominum"
      To Christ who is now in my womb
      Devoutly will I sing.
      Much has the Lord done for me,
      Who is highest in majesty.
      All princes' power he passes by
      As showeth well by this.
      Therefore with heart full and free
      His name always hallowed be,
      And honoured evermore be he
      On high in Heaven's bliss.
      He deposes the mighty from their place,
      And the meek he succoured has.
      The hungry, needy, wanting grace
      With good he has fulfilled.
      The Roman might he has forsaken—

Elizabeth shushes her. Neighbours are uneasy

(*Defiantly*) And to Israel his son taken.
      He——

Elizabeth   Mary, we should make our way
                   To Joseph, thy husband, this I say.
                   Too long hast thou been away.
                   To find him we must speed.

*An Actor comes out of the pageant with a pillow, which Elizabeth and the
Neighbours tie to Mary's belly*

Mary   Cousin, this is good advice.
                   He may suppose me gone amiss.
                   (*She strokes her belly proudly*)
                   Yet God who has ordered this
                   Be witness to my deed.

*An actor playing Joseph comes out of the pageant, L. He has a large false
white beard, which he hooks over his ears, and adjusts before the mirror. He
walks briskly to the front of the pageant, becoming an old man as he rounds the
steps. Mary, signing to Elizabeth and Neighbours to keep a little distance, runs
to him*

Joseph   Mary, my wife so dear.
                   How does thou, dame, and what cheer
                   Is with thee this tide?
Mary   Truly, husband, I am here
                   Our Lord's will to abide.

Joseph embraces her in a fatherly way and discovers the pillow

Joseph   Alas! Alas! What hast thou wrought?
                   Thy body is great. Thou art with child.
                   Never by me thou wast defiled.
                   Therefore, mine is it not.
Mary   The child is fathered where Heaven doth shine.
                   Other father hath he none.
                   I did never sport with man.
                   Wherefore I say, Amend thy moan.
                   The child is God's and thine.
Joseph   "God's child"!
                   God did never play with a maid.
                   And well thou knowest that *I* have never laid
                   Naked with thee entwined.

Elizabeth takes a step forward timidly

Elizabeth   He is God's child. And thine.

Joseph ignores her and addresses the audience

Joseph   God, never let an old man
                   Take to him a young woman.
                   Of this be sure he shall repent.
                   All men may now me despise,
                   Crying, "Old cuckold, thy bow is bent
                   After the new French guise."

Mary indicates to Elizabeth and Neighbours that they should retire to the
pageant. They do so

Mary   Alas, good spouse, why sayest thou thus?
                  Dearest husband, amend thy mood.
                  It is no man but sweet Jesus.
                  He shall be clad in flesh and blood
                  And of thy wife be born.
                  It was an Angel said to me
                  That God's own son in Trinity
                  For man's sake, a man would be
                  To save mankind forlorn.
Joseph   An angel! Oh fie! Oh fie, for shame!
                  To put an angel in such great blame!
                  It was some boy began this game.
                  Well may you him an "angel" name.
Mary   Husband——
Joseph (*to the audience*) Alas, alas! And well-a-day
                  That ever this game betide!
                  That it is true all you may know,
                  Full many a man may hoe the row,
                  Another keeps the bride.
                  So you old men, example take from me.
                  How I am tricked here, well may you see,
                  To wed so young a child.
                  (*To Mary*)
                  And farewell, Mary, I leave thee here alone.
                  Thy person, dame, and all thy works I shun,
                  That have me so beguiled.
                  (*He turns from her*)

Mary goes to sit at the bottom of the steps. L. *Joseph moves a little away, still*
much distressed, talking partly to himself and partly to the audience

                  God's son and mine, she says it is.
                  I will not father it: she says amiss.
                  You, sirs! You! You see my mistake,
                  In old age a wife to take.
                  Alas! Why is it so?
                  To the bishop will I go
                  That he may the law do,
                  With stones her bones to break.
                  (*Second thoughts*)
                  Nay, nay! Let God forbid
                  That I should do that vengeful deed.
                  I never knew in her, so God me speed,
                  A sign of a thing in word or deed
                  That touched villainy.
                  She is meek and mild.

Meek and mild.
(*Third thoughts*)
Yet without man's company
She could not be with child,
And I am sure mine it could never be.
No.
Yet, rather than I should complain openly,
Better it were to leave her,
Forsake this countryside for ever,
And never come in her company.
Since if men knew this villainy,
In scorn they would be hold.
There's many a better man than I
Hath been called cuckold.
(*He reaches the steps, R, and sits wearily down on them*)
Now, Lord God, that all things may
At thine own will both make and dress,
Show me how I may make my way
Through this wilderness.
Here shall I bide until
I shall have slept my fill,
My heart so heavy it is.
(*He sleeps*)

At the steps, L, Mary prays. Gabriel moves over to listen to her prayer

Mary   God that art of my body seized
Thou knowest my husband is displeased
To see me in this case.
By ignorance he is diseased
Therefore, so that he be eased,
Grant him to know thy grace.

Gabriel leaves her and descends a few steps, so as to stand over the sleeping Joseph

Gabriel   Waken, Joseph. And take better care
Of Mary, who is of all wives the best.
Joseph   Oh, I am weary. Let me sleep here.
I have wandered and walked far in this forest.
Gabriel   Rise up, I say, and sleep no more.
Thou makest her heart full sore
That loves thee all the best.
Joseph (*getting up*) Lord, Lord! This is a fair carry-on,
To be wakened and harried from hither and yon,
And nowhere to have rest!
Who art thou? Tell me that thing.
Gabriel   I am Gabriel, God's angel ever.

Joseph   Eh?
Gabriel   God's angel,
                  That has taken Mary into my keeping,
                  And am sent to tell thee God's pleasure.

Joseph kneels

                  In true wedlock you must stay and be.
                  Leave her not. I forbid thee.
                  Nor sin against her ever.

He comes down the steps and raises Joseph

                  But to her fast now thou shalt speed,
                  Nor from her doing naught shalt thou dread.
                  This child that shall be born of her
                  It is conceived of the Holy Ghost.
                  All joy and bliss shall now astir.
                  To mankind shall he be best and most.
                  Jesus thou shalt him call
                  And he shall save his people
                  From troubles and from evil.
Joseph   Ah, Lord God! Benedicite,
                  For thy great comfort, I thank thee
                  That thou hast sent me this grace.
                  (*To the audience*)
                  You should have known forbye,
                  So good a creature as she
                  Would never had done trespass.
                  Now I know well I have ill wrought.
                  I will to mine own poor place
                  And ask forgiveness for my wicked thought.

*He hurries across to where Mary sits. Gabriel watches him then goes back up
the steps, and walks a pace or so across the pageant to be nearer*

                  Say, Mary wife, how farest thou?
Mary   The better, sir, that thou art here.
                  Why standest thou there? Come near.
Joseph   Alas! For joy I quiver and quake.
                  Alas! What foolishness was this?
                  Mercy, gentle Mary, make.
                  Mercy, for I have said all amiss.
                  And all I said I here forsake.
                  Your sweet brow let me kiss.
Mary   Nay, let my brow be. And do you, husband, take
                  My mouth. You may kiss there for thy sake.
                  Welcome art thou to me.

Joseph hesitates, then kisses her. Gabriel draws closer

Joseph   With all my thanks, mine own sweet wife.

With all my heart, my love, my life.
I never shall make more such strife
Betwixt thee and me.
My heart is light now as the wind.
And may he, that can both loose and bind,
And every ill amend,
Teach me grace, power and might,
My wife and her sweet brat
To keep to my life's end.
So, Mary, Mary, while I live
I shall nevermore thee grieve
In earnest or in game.

Mary   Then may our Lord in Heaven, sir, you forgive.
As I do in his name.

Joseph kneels or sits at ground level beside Mary. Gabriel comes down the steps. He/She pauses a little above them, and lifts up one arm, covered with the cloak like a wing, above them in benison. Then he goes on into the pageant

The Lights fade. The Lights come up. Joseph gets up. Time is reckoned to have passed

Joseph (*to the audience*) Lord, what trouble to man is wrought.
Rest in this world he has none.
Octavian, our emperor, hath us besought
To bring our tribute to him. Folk must fare forth.
We are cried in every town and city by name.
I, that am a poor carpenter—though of David's blood, I
    say—
The emperor's commandment I must obey,
Or else I were held to blame.
(*To Mary*)
Now, my wife Mary, what sayest thou to this?
To pay this tribute I must needs wend
To the city of Bethlehem, and far away it is.
Yet to this work I must my body bend.

Mary   My husband and spouse, with thee I shall wend.
A sight of that city fain would I see.

Joseph   My spouse, thou art with child. I fear thee to carry.
For it seems to me a wayward work and wild.
Yet to please thee fain would I,
Since woman are easy to grieve when they be with child.
So let us fare forth as fast as we may,
And Almighty God speed us on our journey.

An actor has come out of the pageant, and goes on his hands and knees to become an Ass. Mary mounts him side-saddle. They proceed to the bottom of the steps, R. The Ass, confronted by the steps, looks outraged, and declines to mount them. Joseph threatens him. Mary stops Joseph from beating the Ass and gets off. Joseph leads her up the steps. The Ass follows

| | Now to Bethelem have we travelled leagues three.
The day is near spent, and draweth unto night.
Fain at thy ease, dame. I would that thou shouldst be,
For you grow aweary—though seemly in my sight. |

Mary   God have mercy, Joseph my spouse so dear.
All prophets hereto do bear witness
That the time now draweth near
When my child will be born, which is King of Bliss.
Unto some place, Joseph, do thou me lead
That I may rest and ease me at this tide.

Joseph sits her down on the rostrum, R. *The Ass stands patiently by*

Joseph   Lo, blessed Mary, here shall ye stay.
The comfort of the Holy Ghost I leave with thee.

An actor leaves the pageant and comes up the steps at L. *He is a citizen on some urgent business. Joseph accosts him*

Joseph   Sir?
Citizen   Sir! (*Continuing*)
Joseph   Sir!
Citizen (*stopping*) Sir?
Joseph   Hail——
Citizen (*continuing*) Hail!
Joseph (*losing his temper*) Hail, worshipful sir, and good day to thee.
A citizen of this city you seem to be.
I look for some harborage for my spouse and me.
For truly this woman is full weary,
And fain at rest would be.
We come at the bidding of our emperor
To pay our tribute and keep ourselves from dolour.
Citizen   Oh, sir, in this town I know no hostelrie
Into which thou or thy wife may get.
The city is beset with people. Sir, I think they lie
Even in the dirty gutters of the street.
Within four walls, sir, sure a place is not
In any house within the city gate.
Even in the street a place may not be sought
Wherein to rest without—at least—debate.
Joseph   Debate?
Citizen   Debate, sir. Of whatever sort.
Joseph   No, sir, debate, that will I not.
All such things are past my power.
And yet my care and all my thought
Are for Mary, my darling dear.
Citizen   Good man, one word to thee I say,
If thou wilt be advised by me.
Yonder is a stable that stands by the way.
Among the beasts, thou yet mayest harboured be.

Citizen points upstage C, *where the tree of life is still set. Joseph goes back to Mary, worried. The citizen follows. Joseph points to where the Citizen had indicated. Mary considers, then nods, and speaks to the Citizen*

Mary Now the Father of Heaven, may he thee shield.
His son in my womb, forsooth he is.
May he keep thee and thine by forest and field.
(*To Joseph*)
Now go we hence, husband, for time it is.

Citizen goes to the tree of life, turns it on its side to make a manger of it, and returns to the pageant by the steps, R. *Joseph leads Mary to the rostrum,* L. *Ass goes first to make a cushion for her*

Hark now, husband. A new relation
Within myself I can feel right well.
Christ in me hath taken incarnation.
Soon will he be born. The truth I tell.
In this poor lodging my chamber I take,
For to abide the blessed birth
Of him that this whole world did make.
Between my flanks I feel he stirreth.

Joseph God be thy help, spouse. It seemeth sore to me,
Thus feebly lodged and in so poor degree,
God's son among the beasts born should be,
This house is desolate without any wall.
Nor fire nor food here is.

Mary Joseph my husband, abide here I shall,
For here shall be born the King of Bliss.
I shall not want or wish for ought.
Almighty God my food shall be.
Now that I am in this chamber brought,
I hope right well my child to see.

Joseph sits on the steps of the rostrum by Mary

An actor who has a fez with a crown round it, or a turban with a crown (securely) fastened to it, comes out of the pageant, R, *adjusts his headgear before the mirror, and walks round the steps to address the audience. He is the 1st King. During his speech, the 2nd King will go through the same routine, and similarly the 3rd King. The 3rd King is old and infirm*

1st King Lord, who lies in everlasting light,
I love thee ever with heart and hand,
That has made me to see this sight
First out of all the people of my land.
They said a star with beams most bright
Out of the East should steadily stand,
And it should be of greater might
Than I that am prince of power in my land,
And should men from sin save.

	So I, who follow it, say,
	God grant that I should have
	Good guidance to find the way.
2nd King	Almighty God, who has all wrought,
	In duty and love I worship thee,
	Who with such brightness hath me brought
	Out of my realm, rich Araby.
	I shall not cease my voyage till I have sought
	What wonderous thing this star may signify.
	God grant me luck so that I might
	Have grace to get good company,
	And my comfort increase
	While this shining star be seen.
	For certainly I shall not cease
	Until I know what it may mean.
3rd King	Lord God that all good hath begun,
	And may all end, both good and evil,
	Who made for men both moon and sun,
	And stayed yon star to stand stone still,
	Till I the cause may clearly know,
	Guide thou me with thy worthy will.
	(*He sees the others*)
	I hope I have some fellows found,
	My yearning faithfully to fulfil.
	Sirs, God keep you in safety,
	And guard you ever from woe.
1st King	Amen! So may it be.
	And save you, sir, also.
3rd King	Sirs, with your will I would you pray
	To tell me some of your intent,
	Wherefore you wend forth in this way,
	And from what country first you went.
2nd King	Full gladly, sir, I to you say,
	A sudden sight to us was sent,
	A royal star that rose by day
	Before us in the firmament,
	That made us fare from home.
3rd King	Why, sirs, I saw the same.
1st King	Sir, of fellowship are we fain.
	Now shall we together wend.
	God grant us, ere we reach the end.
	Some good encouragement to gain.

They cross over the front of the lowest acting area, and pass into the pageant, where they doff their turbans, and are ready to become Shepherds. Meanwhile, Herod, who wears a more elaborate crown like a European king, comes up the step, R, of the pageant, followed by his Herald. Herod stands at the top of the steps. Herald remains in the lower area to address the audience

Herald	All peace, lordlings! Hold you still, Till I have said what I will. Take good heed unto my skill, Both old and young. Herod commands you everyone To hold no king but him alone, And other gods ye worship none, Save Mahomet so free. If ye do else, ye shall be slain; Thus told he me.
Herod	Qui statis in Jude et Rex Israel.
Herald	And the mightiest conqueror that ever walked on ground.
Herod	For I am even he that made both Heaven and Hell, And by my mighty power I hold up this world round. My fearful countenance do the clouds so incumber That oft-times for dread thereof the earth doth shake.
Herald	All the whole world from north to south He may destroy with one word from his mouth.
Herod	Behold but my countenance and my colour, Brighter than the sun in the middle of the day.
Herald	Where could you have a greater succour Than to behold his person, which is so gay?
Herod	My gait and manner, with my gorgeous array— He that had the grace on them always to think—
Herald	Might live always without other meat or drink.
Herod	Now therefore my herald here, called Calchas, Warn thou at every port where ships do arrive, And also every stranger who would through my realm pass, For their passage they shall pay marks five. So speed thee forth hastily, For any who attempts the contrary Upon a gallows hanged shall be, And by Mahomet, of me they get no grace.
Herald	Lord, I am ready at thy bidding To serve thee as my lord and king. For joy whereof, look how I spring, With light heart and fresh gambolling.

He goes off into the pageant, L

Herod	Now shall all regions throughout be sought In every place, both east and west. If any strangers to me be brought, It shall be nothing for their best. (*He comes down the steps*) And for the while that I shall take my rest, Trumpets, viols, and other harmony, Shall bless the waking of my majesty.

He goes into the pageant, R

3rd Shepherd comes out of the pageant, L, playing his pipe and moves freely in the lower area. He is followed by 1st Shepherd (wearing mittens), who addresses the audience. All Shepherds wear sheepskins as cloaks

1st Shepherd   Lord, this weather is cold, and I am ill wrapped.
My legs they fold; my fingers are chapped.
Life goes not as I would. For I am all lapped
In sorrow,
In storms and tempest,
Now by east, now by west,
Woe to him that has never rest,
Nor today, nor tomorrow.
(*He climbs the steps*)
Well, it does me good as I walk thus on my own,
Against this world to make all manner of moan.
To my sheep will I talk and hearken alone.
Then rest on a log, or sit on a stone,
Full soon.
(*He sits down, with his back to the steps*)
For well I dare say,
If true men be they,
I'll have some company
By noon.

2nd Shepherd comes out of the pageant. He is followed by an actor in the company, representing a Sheep. The 2nd Shepherd addresses the audience, then begins to climb the steps. The Sheep decides not to follow, and goes off to keep company with the 3rd Shepherd instead

2nd Shepherd   Benedicite and dominus! What may this mean?
Why fares the world thus? Oft have we seen
These weathers so spiteful, and the wind keen,
And the frosts so hideous they water my een.
No lie!
Now in dry, now in wet,
Now in snow, now in sleet,
And my shoes are freezing to my feet!
It is not all easy.
(*He bumps into the 1st Shepherd*)
1st Shepherd   Look where you're going! Are you deaf, dumb and blind?
2nd Shepherd   The devil take you, with your big behind.
Here, have you seen ought of Daw?
1st Shepherd   I heard his pipe blow
In the low land.
He must be near at hand.
(*He calls*)
Daw!

The Sheep hears and responds

Sheep   Baa!
2nd Shepherd Daw?
Sheep   Baa!
1st Shepherd (*shouting*) Daw!
3rd Shepherd Ah!

He begins to climb the steps, L. *Sheep follows. She grazes at the top of the steps,* R

Now, there was never such floods seen,
Wind and rain so rude, and storms so keen.
Well, God turn all to good: I say as I mean.
And now God save you both, fellows mine.
A drink fain would I, and somewhere to dine.
Shall we sit down together, our bellies to fill?
2nd Shepherd By God, Daw, I will.

As they settle

Let's lay forth our store.
Here's the brawn of a boar.

Unpacking of handkerchiefs containing food to be mimed

1st Shepherd Set mustard before.
Here's the foot of a cow, well sauced I ween
The shank of a sow, that powdered has been.
Two blood puddings, and a dish of liver between.
Now set to, sirs, like brothers together.
There's more.
Both beef and mutton
Of an ewe that was rotten,
Good meat for a glutton.
Eat of this store.
2nd Shepherd I have here in my bag, sodden and roast,
A good ox-tail that would not be lost.
Ha ha!
A good pie, or we fail. This is good for the frost.
Of a swine—two chaps.
Here's a hare in your laps.
We'll need no spoons perhaps.
3rd Shepherd Here, to make up the list, the leg of a goose.
Two glazed chickens. Pork and partridge to roast.
A tart for a lord. How think you this does?
A calf's liver scored, with verjuice.
1st Shepherd Well spoke, by all clergy!
Have some good ale of my mercy.

A bottle is mimed. 2nd Shepherd takes and drinks

Shepherd Here, let not the whole bottle
Go down thy greedy throttle.
(*He takes the bottle and drinks*)

1st Shepherd Close up those lips. Leave me some part.
(He takes and drinks)
Now we must kiss.
2nd Shepherd We'll have a song first.
Who can best sing
Shall take the beginning.
3rd Shepherd Let me take the tenor high.
1st Shepherd I'll to the treble fly.
2nd Shepherd Then the bottom falls to I.

They make ready. 3rd Shepherd gives them the note on his whistle. They open their mouths to sing

But a fourth actor in a ragged cloak has come out of the pageant, R, and begun to climb the steps. This is Mak. As they open their mouths, he begins to sing. They close their mouths again

Mak (*singing*) Now, Lord God, with thy names seven,
That hath made both moon and stars,
How I wish I were in heaven
Where there are no babes
(He searches for a rhyme)
                                        or——
Sheep Baas!
1st Shepherd Who is that who pipes so poor?

Mak, who has been about to grab the Sheep, hastily takes refuge on the rostrum, R, and hides his face with his cloak

Mak A man that comes walking over the moor.
2nd Shepherd Mak, where hast thou been? Tell us thy news.
3rd Shepherd What? Has *he* come? Then take care of your ewes.
Mak What do you mean? I'm a yeoman of the king,
The self and same—son to a great lording.
Et cetera.
Fie on you! Go hence!
Out of my presence!
I must have reverence,
Whoever you are.
1st Shepherd Why act you so quaint? Mak, you do wrong.
2nd Shepherd Don't tell me thou art a saint. I've known thee too long.
Mak Take care, or I'll make a complaint, and then you'll all hang.
At my word.
3rd Shepherd Now, Mak, is that the truth?
Take out that lying tooth,
And set it in a turd.
1st Shepherd (*getting up and threatening him*) And take out that devil that
dwells in thy eye,
Or thee'll get my fist in it. What know you not I?
You do. Or you'll rue.

Mak	Why, of course! It is true.
	I know you.
	You are a . . .
3rd Shepherd	Yes?
Mak	A goodly company.
	All hail to thee.
2nd Shepherd	Shrewd jape!
	(*He sits*)
	And thus late as thou goes
	What will men suppose
	But thou hast an ill nose—
3rd Shepherd	For stealing of sheep.
Mak	I steal sheep! But I am as true as——
1st Shepherd	Steel?

*At the 3rd Shepherd's joke, all three Shepherds fall about with laughter. Mak
tops them. He kneels between, fascinated by so much food*

Mak	Except for a certain sickness I feel.
	My belly's not well; I'm decidedly ill.
	And sore.
	For I've not ate a needle
	This month or more.
1st Shepherd	And how fares thy wife, Mak? How does she go?
Mak	Oh, she lies sweltering by the fireside glow,
	With a house full of brats. And she drinks well also.
	Poor Gil! that's all she really knows how to do;
	Just eat as fast as she can,
	And each year that comes to man,
	She brings forth a little 'un.
	And sometimes two.

*He has attempted to reach out for food, and had his hand slapped. Now 3rd
Shepherd yawns hugely, then the 2nd, then the 1st, each catching a yawn from
the other. Mak begins to move delicately on his knees towards the Sheep*

2nd Shepherd	Now I've watched here as wakeful as any in this shire.
	I must sleep, even though I was to get less for my hire.
3rd Shepherd	I am cold, and ill-clad, and I'd fain have a fire.
1st Shepherd	And I'm weary, exhausted, and covered with mire.
Sheep	Baa!
1st Shepherd (*to 3rd*)	So do you the watch keep.
3rd Shepherd	No, I must go sleep.
	(*To 2nd*)
	You look after the sheep.
2nd Shepherd	My drowse is too deep.
Mak (*standing*)	I'll watch.
Sheep	Baa?

The Shepherds look at him, then at each other

Mak   I shall observe the scene.

Pause

3rd Shepherd   None shall the watch keep.
                   All sleep.
                   And Mak shall sleep between.

*They go to sleep with Mak lying between two Shepherds. The Shepherds begin
to snore*

Sheep   Baa!

*2nd Shepherd has gone to sleep with his head on Mak's legs. When all are
sleeping, Mak sits up cautiously. Very gently he moves 2nd Shepherd's head on
to 1st Shepherd's leg. 2nd is clearly enjoying a very pleasant dream during this
process*

Mak   Now it were time for a man who is bold
                   To steal privily into the fold,
                   And go nimbly to work, for to have and to hold.
Sheep   Baa!

Mary moans and stirs. Joseph crouches by her anxiously

Mak gets to his feet and looks at the snoring Shepherds

Mak   Lord! How they sleep hard.

Louder snore

                   As you can well hear.
                   I was never a sheep-herd, but to learn I'll aspire.
                   (*He approaches Sheep*)
                   Though the flock may be scared, yet I shall nip near.

*A pounce. Sheep tries to Baa! But Mak has his hand over its snout. He picks it
up*

                   Now off homeward we go, and all changes to cheer
                   From sorrow.
                   A fat sheep, I dare say.
                   A fine fleece, I dare lay.
                   So this sheep while I may
                   I will borrow.
                   (*He takes the struggling sheep across the pageant and down the
                       steps at* L. *He shouts*)
                   Ho, Gil! Art thou in? Get us some light.

Gil comes out of the pageant, R. *She wears a head scarf and two sacks across
her shoulders*

Gil   Who makes such a din at this time of night?
Mak   Seest thou not what I bring? (*He puts down the Sheep*)
Gil   Oh, Mak! Mak, my sweeting!

	By thy neck thou wilt swing
	For stealing of sheep.
Mak	Nay? Go away!
	I am worth my meat for I can get
	More than they that work and sweat
	The livelong day.
Gil	It were a foul blot to be hanged for that case,
	For so long goes the pot to the water men says,
	At last
	Comes it home broken.
Mak	I know that token.
	But let it never be spoken.
	So come and help fast.
	There's twelve-month gone past,
	Since I had a taste
	Of sheep meat.
Sheep	Baa!
Mak	I would he were slain. I should like well to eat.
Gil	But what if they follow, and hear the sheep bleat?
Sheep	Baa!
Mak	Ah!
Gil	Now I have spied a scheme, since thou canst none.
	Here shall we hide him until they be gone.
	In my cradle he'll bide. Let me alone,
	And shall lie beside in childbed, and groan.
	This is a good disguise and a far cast.
	Let a woman advise. It helps at the last.
	(*She takes the sheep to the bottom of the steps,* R, *and covers it with the sacks. She sits by it*)
Mak	I'll go back ere they rise. That'll be a cold blast.
	(*He goes back up the steps to the Shepherds. He snores as he approaches*)
	I must be found asleep.
	Still sleeps this company.
	Now to get back between them stealthily.
	As if it had never been I
	That carried off their sheep.
	(*He does so, moving 2nd Shepherd's head back, and begins to snore*)

1st and 2nd Shepherds wake and begin to get up

1st Shepherd	Resurrex a mortuis! Take hold my hand.
	Judas carnas dominus! I may not well stand.
	My foot's asleep. And my throat is like sand.
	(*He sits on the steps of the rostrum,* L *to nurse his foot*)
2nd Shepherd	Ai Eee!
	Lord! I have slept well.
	As fresh as an eel,

As light I do feel
As a leaf on a tree.
(*He jumps*)

3rd Shepherd wakes with a shout

3rd Shepherd Benedicite within. Oh, how my heart quakes.
It near jumps out of its skin with the thump it makes.
Hey! Is Mak here?
(*He gets up quickly*)
2nd Shepherd We were up before thou,
And I give God a vow,
He's gone nowhere.
3rd Shepherd I dreamed he was wrapped in a wolf skin.
While we safely napped, he went out for a spin.
And a sheep he trapped, but he made no din.

Mak snores loudly

1st Shepherd Rise, Mak! For shame! Thou has slept too long! (*He stirs
Mak up a bit with his foot*)

Mary gives a cry, and Joseph takes her hand

Mak Now Christ's holy name be us among.
What's this? By St James, I've got fur on my tongue.
I suppose I'm the same, but my neck has gone wrong.
It's askew.
(*He gets up*)
Small thanks, then, to Heaven.
And I dreamed, by St Stephen.
3rd Shepherd You, too?
Mak I dreamed Gil began to croak, and labour full sad,
And gave birth at first cock to a lively young lad
To add to our flock. Oh, I'll never be glad.
I've got more moss on my rock than ever I had.
Oooh, my head!
A house full of young thanes,
May the devil knock out their brains!
Woe to him that has many bairns
And little bread.
I must go home, by your leave, to Gil now I've thought.
Pray look up my sleeve to see I've stolen naught.
I don't want you to grieve, or from you take ought.
3rd Shepherd Go forth, ere I you heave!

Mak goes off by the steps, L. He waits

Now would I we sought
That we had all our store.
1st Shepherd Then I will go before.

(*He moves a little way to where the Sheep was, and counts. He returns*)

One gone.

Mak   Undo this door! Who's here? How long shall I stand?
                 Gil! What cheer? It is I, Mak, thy husband.

As Gil mimes opening the door, Mary gives a cry

                 The last words that they said when I turned my back
                 Was they'd look if they had all their sheep in the pack.
                 Thou must do as thou planned.

Gil   I accord me theretill.
                 I must swaddle him right
                 (*Tying Sheep's mouth with her scarf*)
                                              in my cradle,
                 And lie down beside.
                 (*Doing so*)
                                      Now help me.

Mak   I will.

Mary moans

Gil   Thou must hear them coming, for they will come anon.
                 Then make ready all, and sing on thy own.
                 Sing lullay thou shalt, for I must groan
                 And cry out by the wall on Mary and John.

Mak   I will.

3rd Shepherd It was Mak or Gil.
                 By St Thomas of Kent!

1st Shepherd Peace, man, be still. I saw when he went.
                 Thou slanderest him ill. Thou ought to repent.

2nd Shepherd Nay, as ever I may speed.
                 It were Mak as did this deed.

They have already started down the steps, L. As they cross the front of the pageant we hear Mary again in labour. Mak begins to sing a lullaby, and Gil to groan. During the ensuing scene there can be much by-play between Gil and the Sheep which is trying to bleat

3rd Shepherd Do you hear anything? A sigh or a groan?

1st Shepherd Heard I never a man sing so clear out of tune.

2nd Shepherd Mak! Open your door soon.

Mak   Who is that speaks as if it were noon
                 Aloft?
                 (*He mimes opening the door*)
                 Good sirs, speak soft.
                 Here is a woman who is not at ease.
                 I'd sooner be dead than if she had any disease.

Gil   Go to another house. I cannot breathe.
                 Each step that you tread

                    Goes right through my head.
3rd Shepherd   You know us, Mak, I think.
Mak (*elaborate recognition*) Why yeay! How fare ye?
                    You've run in the mire; you're still wet.
                    A horse would I hire. Think on it.
                    Sirs, you may see.
                    My dream has come true.

Gil groans, Mary heard after

                    I have bairns if ye knew
                    Far more than a crew,
                    But we must drink as we brew.
2nd Shepherd   Nay, we will neither drink nor eat.
3rd Shepherd   Until our sheep we get
                    As stolen was.
1st Shepherd   Our loss is great.
Mak   Sirs, had I been but there
                    The thief should have bought it full sore.
1st Shepherd   Mak, some men think that you were.

Mary is heard moaning

Mak   Nay, if you suspect my wife and me,
                    Come search our house. Then may you see
                    Who's had her.
                    See if I any sheep got,
                    Or a cow, or bullock.
                    And Gil, my wife, rose not
                    Since down she laid her.
Gil   Out, thieves, from my house.
                    You come to rob us. Out at once.
Mak   Do you not hear her, how she groans?
Gil   Out, thieves, from my barn.
Mak   You do wrong; I you warn.
Gil   Ah! Ah! My middle!
                    I pray to God so mild,
                    If ever I you beguiled.
                    I will eat this child
                    That lies in the cradle.

The Shepherds come to look at Gil. They are in a line by the steps. Mak crouches over the Sheep

Mak   Peace, woman, for God's sake. And weep not so.
                    Thou crackest my brain, and makest me full woe.

The Shepherds lean forward in unison, then back

2nd Shepherd   I think our sheep be slain. What find you two?
1st Shepherd   Our work is all in vain. We may as well go.
                    No cattle here but this, not tame nor wild.

	Our search mistaken is. We are beguiled.
Gil	True as God give me bliss and joy of my child.
2nd Shepherd	Mak, friends will we be. For we are all one.
Mak	Fare thee well, all three.

He shows them out . . . when they are gone

And I am glad you are gone.

The three Shepherds move a little away, then the 3rd speaks to his mates

3rd Shepherd	Fair words there may be, but love there is none.
1st Shepherd	Gave ye the child anything?
2nd Shepherd	Nay, not one farthing.
3rd Shepherd	Then I will back again, If you will be waiting.

Mary is heard. 3rd Shepherd returns and makes as if knocking. Gil starts her groaning again

Mak, take it no grief if I come to thy bairn.

Mak only partly opens the imaginary door, but 3rd Shepherd pushes past him

Mak	No, no. Go away. Thou wilt bring it to harm.
3rd Shepherd	Nay, by your leave, At present I'll give. But sixpence.
Mak	Go away. He sleeps.
3rd Shepherd	I think he peeps.
Mak	When he wakes, he weeps. Go hence.

The other Shepherds come back. Mary is heard

3rd Shepherd	Give me leave him to kiss. I'll lift up the clout. What the devil is this? He has a long snout.
Mak	Takes after me. (*He gets well away from them*)
2nd Shepherd	He is marked all about.
1st Shepherd	May I peep?

Pause

	He is like to our sheep. Will you see how they swaddle His four feet in the middle? Saw I never in cradle A horned lad ere now.
Mak	Peace I say! And let him lie. My wife is his mother. The father am I.
Gil	A pretty child is he. To sit on a woman's knee. A dilly down dilly!

1st Shepherd   I know him by the ear mark. That is a good token.
Mak   I pray you, sirs, hark. His nose was broken.
Gil (*joining Mak*) He was taken by an elf.
                   I saw it myself.
                   When the clock struck twelve
                   He was mis-shapen.

*The Shepherds advance ominously. Sheep has thrown off sacks, and follows.
Gil and Mak retreat*

3rd Shepherd   Since they maintain their theft, they're better dead.
Gil, Mak   No! No!
2nd Shepherd   Two of a kind they be. Peas in a pod.
Gil, Mak   No!
Sheep   Baa!
Mak   Sirs, if I sin again, cut off my head.
1st Shepherd   Now hear my word——

Mary gives a great cry

*Mary's cry freezes and silences them. She cries again. Joseph, who has
surreptitiously loosened the tapes, takes the pillow off her and holds it up. She
stretches out her arms, and he puts the pillow in her arms*

*Gabriel and two Angels appear from the pageant, L, and come up the steps.
They are singing Gloria in Excelsis. All kneel. All look up at them*

Gabriel   Rise, herdsmen, countryfolk!

All rise

                   Now he is born
                   That shall take off the curse which Adam has worn,
                   And shall punish the fiend. This night is he born.
                   God is made your friend now at this morn.
                   To Bethlehem go ye. Hie ye thither in haste.
                   It is his will ye shall him see,
                   Lying in a crib with poor repast.
                   Yet of David's line comes he.

The two Angels retire back into the pageant, L, singing

*The three Shepherds leave Gil, Mak and the Sheep, and began to ascend the
steps, R*

*The three wait until the Shepherds have made the detachment from them, and
then go into the pageant, L*

1st Shepherd   Now follow we the star that shines
                   Till we come to that holy stable.
                   To Bethlehem bend we our ways,
                   And follow on as we are able.
2nd Shepherd   So follow we it that goes forward fast.
                   Such a friend we were loth to fail.

Go on. I will not be the last.
Upon Mary to marvel.

3rd Shepherd Wait now. Go no more steps,
For now the star begins to stand
Hereby. So may it be our hap
That we should see where our saviour be found.

1st Shepherd Soft. Soft. Securely.
Here I see Mary,
And Jesus Christ hard by.

*They approach. Joseph takes the pillow in his arms and places it in the manger.
They kneel in turn to present their gifts*

3rd Shepherd Hail, maid-mother and wife so mild.
As the angel said, so have we found.
I have no present to give to thy child
But my pipe. He may take it, and hold it in his hand,
For much pleasure in playing it I have found.
And now to honour his glorious birth.
He shall have it, to make him mirth.

2nd Shepherd Now hail be thou, child, and thy dame.
For in poor lodgings here art thou laid.
So the angel said, and told us thy name.
Hold, take thou here my hat for thy head.
And now of one thing thou art well sped.
For weather, thou hast no need to complain,
Nor wind, nor sun, nor hail, nor snow, nor rain.

1st Shepherd Hail be thou, Lord, over water and lands.
For thy coming all we may make mirth.
Here, take my mittens to put on thy hands.
Other treasure have I none to present thee with.

Mary Now, herdsmen, countryfolk,
For your coming,
To my child I shall pray,
As he is Heaven's king,
To grant you his blessing,
That you may see again his bliss
At your last day.

The Shepherds sing Gloria in Excelsis, and, still singing, descend the steps at L,
and go into the pageant

Herald comes out of the pageant, R, *with Herod, Herod takes up station at the
top of the steps*

Herald Hail, lord, most of might,
Thy commandment I have done aright,
But into thy land there comes this night,
Three kings in company.

Herod What make they in my country?

| Herald | To seek a king and a child, they say. |
| Herod | A king! |

Herod
On pain of death, bring them this way.
Do it, herald. Hie thee in haste
Before those kings this country shall be past
And in Jerusalem enquire more of that child.

The three Kings come out of the pageant, L, *each carrying a small casket or leather bag*

Herald goes to the Kings

Yet I warn thee, let thy words be mild
There must be care and crafty wiles
How to undo his power. Those kings shall be beguiled

Herald
Hail, sir kings, in your degree.
Herod, king of these countries wide,
Desireth to speak with you, all three,
And for your coming he doth abide.

He presents them to Herod and goes into the pageant, R

1st King
Sir Roi, Regal and Reverent,
Dieu vous garde, omnipotent.

2nd King
Nous sumus venues, coitement,
Nouvelles d'enquerir.

Herod
Soyez bienvenues, rois gentils.
Me dites tont intent.

3rd King
Infant queramus de grand parent
Et Roi de Galilee et Terrae.

Herod
Sirs, advise you what you are saying.
Such tidings make my heart unfree.
I pray you take back those words again
For fear of villainy.
For all men may know and see,
Both he and you, all three,
That I am king in Galilee,
What the devil should this be?
A child, a groom of low degree
To reign above my royalty!

1st King
Sir, we saw a star appear
In the east, bold and clear.

2nd King
But when we came to your land here
Then vanished it away.

3rd King
By prophecies, well know we
That a child born should be
To rule the people of Judee.

Herod
That is false, by my Royalty!
What care I for prophecy?
Prophets' books shall all be torn.
There shall be no king in crown

But I, in my full might.
Who cares for David, that shepherd with a sling,
Esau, Jeremy, with all their offspring?
Here shall there be no Messiah nor king
To expel me from my right.
Yet go ye forth, ye kings three,
And enquire if what is said may be.
But where so'eer ye go, return to me
That I may feast you faithfully.
And if he ye seek be of such high degree,
Well, I will honour him as I will ye
To the full measure of his dignity.

1st King   Then by thy leave, sir, we bid thee good-day
Until we come again this way.

2nd King   Sir, as soon as ever we may,
What we have seen, so shall we say.

3rd King   And all his riches and array
From thee we'll not conceal.

Herod   Then farewell, lords, without delay.
And come back quickly. For your meal.

The Kings bow and retire

Herod comes down the steps to address the audience

By cock's soul! Come they again
All three traitors shall be slain.
And as for that same swaddling swain,
I shall swat off his head.
God's grace shall them nothing gain,
Nor prophecy save them from pain.
And for their clown king—while I reign,
Ruefully runs his rede.

He goes into the pageant, R

The three Kings move towards the bottom of the steps, L

1st King   Yonder, brothers, I see the star.
Whereby I know he is not far.
Therefore, lords, go we near there.

They mount the steps

2nd King   Ah, sirs, I see it stand
Above where he is born.
Lo! Here is the house at hand.

3rd King   Let us make now no more delay.
But take forth our treasury.
And ordained gifts of good array
To worship him as is worthy.

*They approach, 1st **King** advances to rostrum,* R

1st King   Hail! Thou art the fairest of field folk man could find
                 From the fiend and his fellows us to defend.
                 Hail to the best that shall eer be born, and shall unbind.
                 All the bonds that we bear now to an ill end.
                 Hail, child that is come of a king's kind,
                 And shall be king of kith as the prophets have kenned.
                 In token that thou art our king,
                 And shall be aye,
                 Receive this gold, my offering,
                 Prince I thee pray.
                 (*He gives it and retires*)

2nd King replaces him

2nd King   Hail! Food on which thy folk may fully feed.
                 Hail! Fairest flower that shall never fade.
                 Hail! Son that is sent of our Lord's seed,
                 That shall save us of the sin our fathers had.
                 Thou art God's son, most of might,
                 And all ruling.
                 I bring thee incense as is right,
                 For my offering.
                 (*He gives it and retires*)

The 3rd King replaces him

3rd King   Hail! Bairn that is blessed all baleful ills to beat.
                 For our sakes thou shalt be battered and bound.
                 Hail, faithful friend! We fall at thy feet.
                 Thy father's folk from the false fiend thou shalt defend.
                 Hail! Duke that shall drive death underfoot,
                 Yet when thy deeds be done, death is thine end.
                 Bitter myrrh to thee I bring,
                 Since bitter blows on thee shall rain,
                 And thou shalt come to thine ending
                 In bitter death and bitter pain.

Mary   God have mercy, kings, of your goodness.
                 By the guiding of the godhead hither were ye sent.
                 May the power of my sweet son smooth your returning
                 And the Holy Ghost reward you for your presents.

*When Mary finishes speaking, the 3rd (old) King begins to come down the
steps of the rostrum to present his gift. His strength fails and he falls. The
other two Kings help him to rise, and assist him down the steps, L*

1st King   Now, kings, we must keep our promise,
                 And back to Herod we needs must go.
2nd King   Truly, brethren, we can do no less.
1st King   Brethren, you say well. Thus must we do.

Gabriel advances to the edge of the pageant

Gabriel	Ye kings. Stand ye still.

Gabriel
Ye kings. Stand ye still.
Work not after Herod's will.
Herod's fellowship you shall flee.
Your harm ordained has he.
Therefore go not through his country.
The father of good in all things
Has granted you his sweet blessing.
To save you from Herod's punishment
The Holy Ghost this knowledge hath sent.

The Kings look about in amazement. 1st King falls on his kees

1st King
Thanks be to God we honour here
That warns us in this manner.
Else had we gone without care
To him who would us kill.

2nd King
Almighty God in Trinity,
With my whole heart so thank I thee
That sent thine angel to us three
That false foeman for to flee
And so avoid his will.

3rd King
You kings, I tell you, verament,
Since God of his grace us hither sent,
We will do his commandment,
Whatever may befall.
Therefore stand we not in doubt,
But go to walk our lands about,
And of his birth we'll not stand mute,
But tell it to great and small.

They go into the pageant, L

Gabriel turns to Joseph and Mary

Gabriel
Joseph, arise! And that anon.
Into Egypt thou must be gone,
And Mary also with her son.
That is my Lord's will.
There stay, lest this child be slain,

Mary quickly takes the cushion from the manger

Till I warn thee to come again.
For Herod, the false king, is fain
God's blood for to spill.

Joseph
But, lord, what ails the king at me,
For him I never did offend?
Alas, what ails him for to kill
A small young bairn that neer did ill
In word nor deed against his will?
This is an ill affair.

> I am an old man and sere.
> My bones are bruised and bare.
> It is too much. I would it were
> My last day, and all at end.
> Besides, I do not know the way,
> How we shall wend.

Gabriel Joseph! Joseph!
> Company I shall you bear
> Until you find your harbour there.

Joseph (*helping Mary to rise*) Then, Mary, to Egypt we must flit.
> Thou upon mine ass shalt sit.

Ass gets into position in front of the rostrum

> Rise up, hastily and soon.
> Our Lord's will must needs be done.

Mary Meekly, Joseph, my own spouse,
> Towards that country let us repair.
> And find in Egypt a new house.
> God grant us grace to come safe there.

Mary mounts the Ass. It carries her to the top of the steps, L, Joseph leading it. When it gets there, it looks at her beseechingly, and she gets off, and goes down on foot, Joseph helping. The Ass follows

Gabriel watches them go, then turns to look R, as:

Herod comes out of the pageant, R, mounts the steps and goes to the rostrum

Gabriel goes down the steps, L, and into the pageant

Herald comes out of the pageant, R, to the bottom of the steps

Herald Hail, Herod king, worthiest in deed!
> Hail, maintainer of courtesy through all this world wide!
> Hail, mightiest king that ever bestrode a steed!
> Hail, the manliest man in armour to abide!
> Hail——

Herod Yes?

Herald Lord, those three kings that forth were sent
> And should have come again,
> Contrary to thy clear commandment
> Another way have ta'en.

Herod Another way! Out! Out! Out!
> Have those false traitors done me this deed?
> I stamp. I stare. I look all about.
> Might I them take, they to the fire should speed.
> I rant. I rave. If I could run, I would.
> These villain traitors have marred my mood.
> They shall be hanged if I can them come to.
> As for the beast of Bethlehem, he shall be dead,

And thus I shall the prophecy fordo.
(*Calling*)
How now! Awake out of your sleep,
Sir Grimbald and Sir Launcher deep!

Two sleepy Knights with wooden swords come out of the pageant, L, *and go up the steps to Herod*

Herald goes into the pageant, R

How say you, knights? Is not this the best word?
You shall slay all young children with the sword.

1st Knight What?

Herod Slay all young children with the sword.
Therefore, my knights, good and keen,
Be lively! Go work out my spleen.
Slay that young shrew. Slay all. Let it be seen
That you be men of main.
Drive out the dirty arses one by one
So that they all be slain.

1st Knight Alas, lord and king of bliss,
Sent you after us for this?
A villainy it were I guess
For my fellow and me
To slay a shitten-arsed crew.
A peasant could do this barbecue.
We are not cut-throats or some such brew
But knights of good degree.

2nd Knight Well said, good comrade! And so say I.
Sir king, if you persevere in this way.
To see so great a murder of young fry
Will make a rising in thine own country.

Herod A rising! Out! Out! Out!
Out, villain wretches! Out on you, I cry.
Look that you wreak my will and utterly,
Or on a gallows both of you shall die.
You shall walk both far and near
To Bethlehem, and spare no little dear.
All boy children, within two year,
And one day old,
You shall slay them, one and all.
So shall you rid me of one who would call
My wealth, my kingdom, crown and all
Into his fold.

The Knights look miserably at each other, and back at Herod

1st Knight Well, cruel Herod, we shall do this deed.
Since your will in this kingdom must needs be wrought.
All children of that age, die they must need.

2nd Knight   And I will swear here, upon my bright sword,
                   All children that I find, slain they shall be.
                   Thus many a mother will weep, and be affraught,
                   When they shall see us riding in our panoply.
Herod   Now you have sworn, forth do ye go,
                   And work my will both day and night.
                   When all be dead, return before my sight.
                   Then will I gambol like a little doe.

The Knights go down the steps and mount imaginary horses

*Three women, each carrying a pillow for a child, come out of the pageant, L,
one after another*

1st Knight rides C to meet the first

1st Woman (*singing*) Be still, be still! My little child!
                   The Lord of lords save thee and me.
                   For Herod has sworn with words so wild
                   That all young children, slain they shall be.

1st Knight gets off his horse

1st Knight   Say, widows and wives, whither are you away?
                   What you bear in your arms, needs must we see.
                   If they be man-children, die they must this day,
                   Since at King Herod's will, all things must be.
1st Woman   Sir knights, of your courtesy,
                   This day shame not your chivalry.
                   But on my child have pity
                   For my sake at this tide.
                   A simple murder it were to hew
                   A child's limbs to work him woe,
                   That can neither speak nor go,
                   Nor ever harm did.
1st Knight   Dame, abide. And let me see
                   A boy child if that be.
                   The king, he has commanded me (*taking the pillow*)
                   All such should (*stabbing*) arrested be.

*1st Woman gives a great cry and grabs the pillow back. But the child is dead.
She goes off sobbing into the pageant, R. As she goes*

1st Woman   My long lulling is now forlorn.
                   Alas! Why was my bairn born?
                   With swinging sword now is shorn
                   His head from off his neck.
                   Shank and shoulder is all torn.
                   Sorrow I see, both hither and yon,
                   At midnight, midday, and at morn.
                   My life no more I reck.

She goes into the pageant, R

2nd Woman makes a dash, R. *2nd Knight intercepts*

2nd Knight   Come hither to me, Dame Parnell.
          And show me here thy son, Snell.
          For the king has bid me quell
          All that we find male.

2nd Woman   Be thou so hardy, I tell thee straight,
          To handle my son that is so sweet,
          My distaff and thy head shall meet.
          And that shall make thee quail.

2nd Knight   Dame, thy son, in good fay,
          He must learn of me a play.
          He must hop before I go away.
          (He stabs the pillow on the word "hop")

2nd Woman   Out! Out on thee, thief!
          My love, my lord, my dear, my life!
          Never did man or woman grieve
          To suffer such torment.
          Yet revenged I shall be.
          Have here one! two! and three! *(Attacking him)*
          Bear these to the king from me.
          And tell him from whom they're sent.

She attacks the Knight, who hastily mounts his horse and rides back into the pageant, R, *pursued by the 2nd Woman*

1st Knight approaches the 3rd woman, whose pillow has a purple cover

1st Knight   Dame, show me thy child here.
          He must hop upon my spear.
          If he a little dangler bear,
          I shall teach him a play.

3rd Woman   Nay, freak, thou shalt fail.
          My child thou shalt not assail.
          He has two holes under his tail.
          Kiss them if you may.

1st Knight   Faugh!

He twists the neck of the pillow and throws it down

A long laugh. Scorn and delight

3rd Woman   Out! Out! Out! Out!
          You shall be hanged, all the rout.
          Thief, be you never so stout,
          Full foul you have done. *(She picks up the pillow)*
          This child was given to me
          To look to. Thieves, woe be ye!
          He was not mine, as you shall see;
          He was the king's son.

1st Knight   Oh!

3rd Woman   I shall tell King Herod while I may

His child was slain before my eyes.
Thief, you shall be hanged high
When I my tale have done.

1st Knight falls back, horrified and goes into the pageant, L

3rd Woman mounts the steps, R, *and comes to Herod, holding the pillow before her*

	Look, lord. Look and see.
	This child thou gave to me,
	Men of thine own company
	Have slain him. See him dead.
Herod	Fie, whore, fie! God give thee pain.
	Why didst thou not say the child was mine.
	Vengeance! Vengeance! As drink I wine,
	Vengeance upon each head!
3rd Woman	Yea, lord. Thou sayst aright.
	Thy son was like to have been a knight.
Herod	He was clad in silk array,
	In gold and purple that was so gay.
	They might well know. They might know
	He was a king's son.
	What the devil! Didst thou not say?
	Woman why were thy wits away?
	Couldst thou not speak? Couldst thou not pray?
	And say it was my son?
	(*He comes down the steps,* R)

The Lights fade on the pageant, and on all but the area already used for Cain and Satan

Alas! Alas! My days are done!
Now come I to die soon,
And damned I must be.
My legs are rotting, and my arms.
I have done so many harms.
Now I see the devil's swarms
Coming from hell for me.
I bequeath here in this place
My soul to be with Satanas.
I die! I die! Alas! Alas!
My son is dead, and I must pass.
I die!
(*He begins to scream and rave. It should be as frightening as
possible, as mad as possible, loud and out of control*)

The Lights fade to Black-out

*Over the Black-out, from the door of the hall, a cry of "Peanuts!" "Ice-
cream!" "Lemonade!"—anything at all from beer to chicken-legs, whatever*

the local authorities will allow to be sold in the auditorium or the doorway. *The effect should be of sharp interruption of the action by the demands of ordinary life. Full stage and auditorium Lights come up at the interruption by the vendors. Herod and the 3rd Woman go to get a drink, ice-cream or whatever, and go on into the pageant*

END OF ACT I

ACT II

During the interval, the Act I props are struck, and those for Act II set. The tree of knowledge is struck and a large cross is set in the corner of the steps, R. The actors will assist the stage management in the striking and resetting of props, and will return to their places in the pageant just before the interval ends

House lights lowered. Full stage lights on

Satan comes out of the pageant, L, adjusts his mask, and advances to speak to the audience. During his speech he will mount to the top of the pageant so that he may observe the action for a while

Satan

I am your lord Lucifer, that out of Hell came,
Prince of this world and great Duke of Hell.
I am nourisher of sin, to the confusion of man,
To bring him to my dungeon, there in fear to dwell.
Thus shall I reward him. For sin he gets this gain,
To sing welladay for ever, and sit in the skin of pain.

For I began in Heaven sin for to sow
Among all the angels that were there so bright.
Therefore was I cast out into Hell full low
Notwithstanding I was the fairest and bearer of light.
Take heed to your prince, then, my people every one,
And see what mischiefs in Heaven I can play.
To get a thousand souls an hour I think but scorn.
Why! I was with Adam and Eve on the first day.

But now memories of marvels run into my remembrance,
Of one, Christ, of Joseph's name, and Mary's son.
Thrice I tempted him by right subtle instance,
After he had fasted for forty days (against all sensual reason)
High I put him on a pinnacle, but angels were to him assistant.
I came but to vainglory, and lost mine intent.

Jesus with Magdalene, Judas, John, Peter, James and Philip in attendance, comes out of the pageant, L. Magdalene carries a vial, supposed to contain ointment. Jesus is dressed all in white, all the disciples except Judas have haloes. Jesus sits on the steps, L, with the disciples at a little distance. Magdalene pours the (imaginary) contents of the vial over his head and shoulders. Then she massages it in. Meanwhile

Now he hath twelve disciples to attend him.
To the folk of town and city he will send them.
Over the crooked, blind and dumb his spirit prevails.
Lazarus, that for four days lay dead, he to life restored.
And where I purpose to tempt, there he assails.
Magdalene, who craved remission, had it at his word.
But now the time draws nigh of his persecution.
I shall devise new engines of malicious conspiracy.
I shall provide reproofs to his confusion,
And I shall falsify the words his people testify.
His disciples shall forsake him, and their master deny.
Innumerable shall his wounds be, of woeful grievance.
A traitor shall contrive his death to fortify.
All the rebukes he gave me shall turn to his displeasance.
Thus shall I be revenged. In trust is treason.
Better to work with cunning and discretion.

Magdalene has finished. The vial is on the steps

John   Sir, where will you eat your Pascal feast?
             Tell us. That we may prepare it best.
Jesus   Go forth, John and Peter, to yon city.
             When you come there, then you shall see
             In the street a man,
             Bearing water in a can.
             To him you shall speak and say
             That I come here by the way.
             Say I pray him, if his will it be,
             But for a little while give ease to me,
             That I and my disciples all
             May rest within his hall.
Peter   Lord, we shall go to that city.
             Your Pascal feast shall ordered be.

A Man, bearing a water jar, comes out of the pageant, R

John and Peter advance to meet him

             Sir, our master the prophet,
             Comes behind us in the street.
             And for a chamber he you prays
             To eat and drink and take his ease.
Man   Sirs, he is welcome unto me.
             And so is all his company.

The Man leads them back towards the pageant, treating the entrance as a door

             Sirs, walk in at the door,
             And see what victuals I may offer you.
             I am so glad that you have come before,
             I do not know what joy may make me do.

He takes John and Peter into the pageant

Jesus rises and moves forward, the others following except for Judas

Jesus   My path is hard—by holy ordinance,
Which shall convey us all where we must go.
And now full ready is the purveyance
Made by my friends out of their love, I know.
Containing our souls in peace, now proceed we.
For love of man this way I take.
For with my inward eye, I truly see
That man for man must the amendment make.

All but Judas go into the pageant

Satan watches Judas. He comes down the steps, picks up the vial and gives it to him on the word "unguent", after which he goes into the pageant, L

Judas   By dear God in majesty,
I am as angry as may be.
And some way I will vent it out of me,
As soon as ever I may.
My master, Jesus, as men may see,
Anointed was, head, foot and knee,
And with an unguent more dainty
Than I saw for many a day.
Had I of it had mastery,
I would have sold it thriftily
And put it in our treasury.
Three hundred pennies worth it was,
That he let spill in that place.
Therefore God give me hard grace,
Himself he shall be sold
To the Jews, or I lie,
For the tenth part of that money.
Thereby will I be quit of my envy
And grief a hundredfold.

Pilate comes out of the pageant, R, *followed at a discreet distance by Caiphas and Annas. Two Knights and a Doctor come out,* L. *The two Knights carry wooden swords, and the Doctor wears a gown. Caiphas and Annas wear cardinals' hats. A Porter follows a little behind,* R. *He wears a long apron (he will be a double for Jesus), and takes his place at the foot of the steps,* R, *while Pilate goes on up to the rostrum and the rest place themselves on the pageant. Judas remains where he is*

Pilate   Under the royallest king of riches and renown,
Now am I regent, to rule this region in rest.
Unto my bidding must bishops be bound,
And bold men that in battle fight breast to breast.
To my care is entrusted this tower-girt town.

Traitors will I attaint, the truth to trust.
Pontius Pilate, of three parts,
Then is my proper name.
Among philosophers first
Got I my fame.
And thus since we stand in our state,
You lords of place in this land,
Tell us, if you have wit and know't,
Whether there be ought of sorrow or debate
That needs to be handled full haste,
Since all your help hangs in my hand.

Caiphas   Sir, to certify the truth in your sight,
As you are our sovereign, it is seemly to seek.

Pilate   Why? Is there any mischief-maker musters his might?
Or malice through mean men?

Annas   Sir, there is one rank swain,
Whose rule is not right.
And through his rumour in this realm
Has raised a great reek.

Pilate   But why are ye both thus deranged?
Be ruly and lay forth the reason.

Caiphas   Sir, what he teaches is strange.

Annas   We seek for your succour this season.

Pilate   If that wretch in our ward
Hath wrought any ill,
Since we are warned, we would know,
And ere we go, we will.
But if his teaching be lawful,
Do not false witness bear.
We shall allow him, if he will,
To dwell in love here.

Doctor   If that false traitor
Your forbearance may find,
I see well that our folk
May fail of a friend.
For he teaches the people to call
Him God's son. And he says that he shall
Sit in Heaven, for there is his hall.

Pilate   And what if that force to him fall?
If he should be indeed
The one that you said should descend
To succour yourselves and your seed?

Caiphas   Ah, soft, sir! And cease.
Of Christ when he comes, no kindred shall be known.
But of this caitiff's kin we know the increase.

Annas   He likens him to be like God in throne.
And the burdens of this world he shall release.

Doctor   If you will, sir, you may know,

	He is least worthy of men.
	In our temple he has taught
	Times more than ten.
	Where tables full of treasure lay
	To count and try
	Of our chief money-changers
	He cast them out thereby.
1st Knight	Aye! And skelped out a score
	That stately stood there, selling their store.
Pilate	And what taught he there?
1st Knight	Sir, that our temple is the tower
	Of his enthroned sire.
	There should we praise him whose might is set o'er
	Both prince and Empire.
Pilate	Ah ... But is he not mere mad?
	Sure your rancour is raw.
Caiphas	Sir, he would loose our law,
	And on the sabbath the sick would he save,
2nd Knight	Healing all who would come
	Recovery to crave.
	He holds not our holy days.
	Hard fortune may he have.
	Let him be hanged by the neck.
Pilate	Hold, sirs! A pause is needy.
	To drive him guiltless to his grave
	Be not so greedy.
	Without grounds you gain little.
	Look your petition be legal,
	Without any trifles to tell.
Caiphas	He perverts our people who approve his preaching.
	For that point you should press his power to impair.
Annas	He calls himself king,
	And therefore our commons are cast into care.
Pilate	King?
2nd Knight	King.
Pilate	If so be, then that jest to sorrow shall him bring,
	And he shall curse the bones that did him bear.
	That wretch from our wrath shall not wring
	Ere wrack be wrought on him.
Caiphas	So would we that it were.
Annas	So you should sustain your zeal.
Pilate	Well, know ye this work shall be done,
	And the knave be taught to kneel.

Judas makes his mind up, goes to the foot of the steps, R, and raps on the cross which does duty for a gate

Judas	Open, porter, the gate of this proud place
	That I may pass to your princes.

Porter	Go hence, staring vagabond. God grant thee ill grace,
	You've treason about you, I see in your face.
Judas	Good sir, pray be quick. I've tidings to tell.
Porter	Mars has morticed his mark
	On thy face, I see well.
	Thou art a strange thief and stark.
	To mar men of might hast thou marked in thy mind.
	I shall work thee some woe, if away thou'lt not wend.
Judas	Ah, good sir, take heed
	To my talking this tide.
	True tidings I tell.
	If my truth be tried,
	To mirth it shall lead.
	And your dukes by my deed
	(*He bribes him by giving the vial*)
	From dread shall be drawn.
	Come I but to council,
	And my cause shall be known.
Porter	Bide here, my dear.
	Before more boasts be blown
	Or seeds be sown,
	I'll to our sovereign lords,
	Where banners are bright,
	And say a fellow such as thou
	Sues to their sight.
	(*He mounts the steps*)
	Oh, my lord, that is so well of wit,
	There's one in suit. I come to tell of it.
Pilate	Speak on.
Porter	A hynd full of ire, and hasty he is,
	With a keen face, uncomely to kiss.
Pilate	Get him that his complaint may now be known.
	No open language comes to us amiss.

The Porter goes down and motions Judas up the steps. Then he himself goes off into the pageant, R

Judas	May that lord, sirs, sustain your zeal,
	Who is the flower of fortune and fame.
Pilate	Welcome. Thy words are well.
Caiphas (*to Judas*)	Thou knave! Canst thou not kneel?
Pilate (*to Caiphas*)	Let be, sir, your scorning, for shame!
	(*To Judas*)
	And you, sir, be not abashed to bide at the bar.
Judas	Sirs, I that am before you brought
	Have been about and about.
Annas	And saw what?
Judas	Work, sirs, that hath been wrought
	Against your content.

Now I would make a merchandise
This mischief to prevent.
For if you will bargain or buy,
Jesus I will sell.

Pause

Annas   My blessing. Your bargain is well.
Doctor   Lo, here is a sport to spy!
Judas   And him shall I promise you soon
If you will be quick to my plot.
Pilate   Tell me what is thy name?
Judas   Judas Iscariot
Pilate   Thou art a just man.
Bid forth thy bargain.
Judas   A little payment, no more,
To take from this hall.
Pilate   How much?
Judas   Thirty pence is all.
Pilate   Sirs, are you pleased at this price?
Caiphas (*producing a money bag*) Since Judas knows him culpable.
Else were our consciences too nice.
Pilate   Say, man, to sell thy master
What hath he moved amiss?
Judas   He wasted money. Ten times more than this.
1st Knight   How shall we know him?
Judas   Take that caitiff whom I kiss.

They fall away a little from him. He looks from one to another, then turns and goes swiftly down the steps. Pilate signs to the two Knights, who follow him. All three go into the pageant, R

Caiphas   When we have reached the reckless pest,
His ribs shall we rap.
Annas   And make that "king" before we rest
To run and rave and leap.
Pilate   No, sirs. You shall not scourge him
Or mortify his shape.
For if the fool be blameless,
It suits us him to save.
Therefore when you shall go to get him
Unto his body do no ill.
Annas   In your sight, sound shall we set him.
Pilate   So may you keep safe your soul.

Pilate goes down the steps, the others following, and into the pageant, R

Jesus comes out of the pageant, L, *followed, as fast as they can make the change, by the actors playing Peter—who carries a sword—James and John*

Jesus   Now my dear friends and brethren each one,

Remember these words that I shall say.
The time is now come that I must be gone
For to fulfil the prophecy.
Man is my brother. Him I may not forsake,
Nor show him unkindness by no way.
In pains for him, my body shall shake,
And for love of man, the son of man shall die.
So now I warn you, my friends free,
List to these lessons that I say.
The fiend is wrath with you and me,
And he will mar you if he may.
But, Peter, I have prayed for thee
So that thou shalt not dread his dree,
And comfort thou shalt this company,
And guide them when I am gone away.

Peter   Nay, Lord, it shall not be so.
My life I will put in woe
And for thy sake be slain.

Jesus   Peter, I tell thee truthfully,
Ere the cock hath crowed, one, two, and three,
Thou shalt forswear my company,
And take my word again.
Brethren, let not your hearts be sore,
But live in God evermore
And in me as you have before,
And grieve not for this case.
For in my father's house there is
Many a mansion of great bliss,
And thither my fate to go it is
To make for you a place.

They have reached the foot of the steps, R

Peter, with thy fellows, here shalt thou abide,
And watch till I come again.
I must make my prayer here at this tide.
My flesh quaketh for fear and pain.

Peter   Lord, thy request doth us constrain.
We shall not move until thou comest again.

Jesus goes up the steps and kneels by the rostrum, L. *Meanwhile*

Yeah, sirs, I say unto you.
Sit we down on this hillside.
Here let us rightly take our rest.
My bones are heavy as any lead.

John   And I must sleep. Down shall I lie.

James   In faith, fellows. So fare I.
I may no longer hold up my head.

They sit on the steps and go at once to sleep. Jesus prays

Jesus　　Oh, Father, Father, for my sake,
This great passion take from me,
Which is ordained I must take
If man's soul saved should be.
My heart is in great misliking
For death that is to me coming.
Father, if I dare ask this thing,
Put it away from me.
(*He rises. Returning to the top of the steps*)
Unto my disciples will I go again.
Kindly to comfort them, who are couched in care.
What? Are you fallen asleep now, everyone?
And might you not have watched for but one hour?

The Disciples stir and moan. Jesus walks a little away

Father in Heaven, I beseech thee,
Remove my pain by thy great grace,
And let me from this death flee,
Since I never did any trespass.
Everything to thee possible is.
Nevertheless, now in this
At your will I am, I guess.
As thou wilt, let it be.
(*Getting no answer to his prayer, he turns again to look at the
Disciples*)
Peter, Peter, thou sleepest fast.
Awake thy fellows, and sleep no more.
Of my death, are ye not aghast?
You take your rest, and I suffer sore.
(*He goes back to the rostrum, L, and kneels*)
Father, the third time I come again
To ask deliverance of this pain.
For thy son's sake, Father, hear this cry.
Thou knowest that I never did but good.
It is not for me, this death that I must die,
But for man that I sweat both water and blood.

An Angel comes out of the pageant, L, and up the steps

Angel　　Hail, both god and man indeed.
Thy father bids thee, thou should not dread,
But fulfil his intent
As the Parliament of Heaven hath meant.
That man's soul should now redeemed be
From Heaven to earth, Lord, thou wert sent.
That deed pertaineth unto thee.

Jesus rises

Jesus   Father, thy will fulfilled shall be
There is nought to say against this case.
I shall fulfil the prophecy,
And suffer death for man's trespass.

He returns to the Disciples. The Angel remains to watch

You sleep, brethren, yet I see.
Sleep on now, all of ye.
My time is come, taken to be.
From you I must away.
He that hath betrayed me,
This night from him will I not flee.
In a sorry time born was he.
And so he may well say.

Judas comes out of the pageant, L, followed by two Knights and the Doctor

The Disciples wake. Moment of confrontation

You men, I ask. Whom seek ye?

1st Knight   Jesus of Nazareth. Him seek we.

Jesus   Here, all ready. I am he.

Judas pushes through the others, mounts the steps, and kisses him

Judas   Welcome, Jesus, my master dear.
I have sought thee in many a place.
I am full glad I find thee here.
For I knew not where thou wast.

Jesus   Judas, why dost thou such deceit?
Can you not tell I know thy will?
By that kiss shall I be forfeit.
Yet you shall rue it in time, full ill.
(*To Knights*)
Now, whom seek ye with weapons keen?

Angel clears by the steps, L, and into the pageant

1st Knight   To tell the truth, and not to lie,
We seek Jesus the Nazarene.

Jesus   I said before that it was I.

The Doctor has a loop of rope and is officious. He begins to bind Jesus's hands

Doctor   Dare no man on him lay hand.
I shall catch him if I may.
(*To Jesus*)
A flattering fool hast thou been long.
But now has come thine ending day.

Peter   Thief! And thou be so bold,
My master for to hold,
Thou shalt be quit a hundredfold.

58 The Fall and Redemption of Man

He swipes at the Doctor's ear with his sword. 1st Knight engages Peter in combat. 2nd Knight restrains the other two Disciples

Doctor   Ahooooh!
Peter   So take thou that, bold wight.
Thy ear hast thou lost, by God's grace.
Go! Now complain to Caiphas,
And bid him do thee right.
Doctor   Out! Alas! Alas! Alas!
By cock's bones, my ear he has.
Jesus   Peter, put up thy sword on high.
(He takes it and gives it to 1st Knight)
Who so with sword shall smite gladly
By sword shall perish hastily.
(To Doctor)
Thou, man, that moans thy hurt so sore,
Come hither. Let me thy wound see.
Take of me the ear that Peter shore.
In nomine patris, whole thou be.
Doctor   Ah, well is me! Ah, well is me!
My ear is healed now as I see.
1st Knight   Yet though he has healed thee,
Safe from us he shall not be.
But to Sir Caiphas go shall he.

1st Knight puts his sword on Jesus's left shoulder to restrain him, while 2nd Knight binds Jesus's hands. Disciples keep their distance

Jesus   As to a thief you come here,
With swords, and staves, and full armour,
To take me in a foul manner,
And work your wicked will.
In the temple was I with you aye.
No hand on me then would you lay.
But now is come the time and day
Your talent to fulfil.
1st Knight   Lead him forth fast out of the gate,
And hanged be he that spares him ought.
2nd Knight   Out of our hands, thou shalt not pass,
For all the craft thou can.
Till thou come to Sir Caiphas,
Save thee shall no man.

They lead him up on top of the pageant by the steps, L. Judas looks from Peter, to John, to James, who gaze at him in horror. He breaks from them, and goes into the pageant, R. The three Disciples follow the procession as far as the foot of the steps, L

Magdalene comes out of the pageant, R, and sees the Disciples. She crosses to them. John takes her hands in his and points up the steps. The Disciples go into the pageant. Mary comes out of the pageant, R. Magdalene goes to her

Magdalene   Oh, immaculate mother, of all women most meek,
Oh, devoutest in holy mediation ever abiding.
The cause, dear lady, that I your person seek
Is to know if you have any tiding
Of your sweet son and my reverent Lord, Jesu,
That was your daily solace, your holy consolation.

Mary   I would you should tell me, Magdalene, if you know,
For to hear of him is all my affection.

Magdalene   I would fain tell, lady, yet I must be weeping.
For sooth to the Jews he is sold.
With cord they have bound his hands, and have him in
keeping.

Mary   Ah, how my heart is cold.
Jesu! Jesu! Jesu! Jesu!
Why shouldst thou suffer this tribulation and adversity?
How may they find it in their hearts thee to pursue,
That never trespassed in the last degree?
Thy every thought and deed to good did pass.
Therefore why shouldst thou suffer this great pain?
I suppose verily it is for my trespass.
And. oh, I wish my heart might break in twain.
Oh, father of Heaven, where be thy behests
Thou promised me when a mother thou me made?
Thy blessed son I bore among the beasts,
And now the bright colours of his face do fade.
Oh, good father! To will that his son should suffer so!
Who never disobeyed thy precept or could be admonished!
And has to every creature pitiful been, and gentle as I know.
And now for these kindnesses is most painfully punished.
(*She turns and looks upward to where Jesus stands at the top of
the pageant*)
Now, dear son, since thou hast ever been so full of mercy,
And will not spare thyself, for the love thou hast to man.
On all mankind now have pity,
And think on Mary, thy mother, that heavy woman.

Mary and Magdalene go into the pageant, L

1st Knight (*calling*) Sir Bishops!

Annas and Caiphas come out of the pageant, R, and mount the steps, as

Sir Bishops, here have we brought
A wretch that much woe hath wrought,
And would bring our law to nought.

Annas   Ah, jangling Jesus, art thou here?
Now mayest thou prove thy power.
Whether thy cause be clean and clear,
Thy Christhood we shall know.

Caiphas   Methinks if he a magician were,

	Either for a penny or a prayer He should shunt himself out of this danger, And give the world a show.
Annas	Now thou art brought here, and stand us before. Say why thou hast troubled us, and subverted our law.
Caiphas	Who are thy disciples that follow thee about? And what is thy doctrine that thou dost preach? Tell me now of this and bring us out of doubt That we may to other men thy preaching teach.
Jesus	At all times have I preached. Openly it was done, In the synagogue or in the temple where all the Jews come Ask them what I have said, and also what I have done. They can tell my words. Ask them, everyone.
1st Knight	Sir Caiphas, hearken unto me. This babbler our king would be. Whatever he says now before thee, I heard him say in time of yore That he could work so powerfully, Destroy the temple well might he, And build it up in days three, Trim as it was before.
2nd Knight	Yes, verily, so I heard him say. He may deny it in no way. And that he was God's son as well, Messiah and Emmanuel.
Caiphas	What sayest thou now, Jesus? Why answerest thou not? Hearest thou not what is said against thee? Speak, man, speak. Speak, thou fop. Hast thou scorn to speak to me? Now I charge thee and conjure thee by sun and moon. Tell us in truth an' if thou be God's son.
Jesus	As thou sayest, so say I I am God's son, Almighty. And here I tell thee truly That me thou shalt see Sit by God's hand on high, Mankind in heaven to justify.

Three Citizens come out of the pageant, R, and stand at the bottom of the steps, hoping to see what is going on. Peter is behind them, unwilling to be recognized

Caiphas	Out! Alas! What is this? Hear ye not how he blasphemeth God? What need we for more witness Than you have heard at his own word? Think ye not he is worthy to die?
Doctor Knights Citizens	*(shouting)* Yeay! Yeay! Yeay!

Annas	Bear him away, and beat him heartily,
	That he may suffer for his blasphemy.
1st Knight	You heard in this place
	How the fellow hath lied.
	In the middle of his face
	Will I spit betide.

He sits and pushes Jesus towards the top of the steps, R. *Then he goes on to the bottom of the steps*

2nd Knight	Fie on thee, freak!
	Thy bones will I break.

A punch and a push

Doctor	If thou be Christ,
	And loth to lie,
	Then who smote thee,
	Testify.

A punch and a push. Jesus is now at the top of the steps

2nd Knight	For all his prophecy,
	Yet he fails totally.
	Say, canst thou dodge——

He pushes Jesus down the steps

1st Knight	Where my fist shall lodge?

He catches Jesus and punches him.

Laugh. Jeering. The two Knights and the doctor run Jesus across the front of the pageant, L. *The Knights throw him down on the ground, where he lies*

The Doctor spits at him scornfully and goes into the pageant, L. *So do two Citizens*

Caiphas and Annas have come half-way down the steps, R, *to watch what is going on. A woman (who is the third Citizen) hangs back, and does not follow her fellows*

Jesus looks up and sees Peter. A long exchange of glances. Then Jesus smiles, sadly, and turns away. The Woman looks from Jesus to Peter

Woman	What thinkst thou how they treat this man?
	Art thou not his disciple? He did regard thee then.
Peter	Woman, I never saw the man.
	Never, since the world began.
Woman	Sayst thou?
	(She looks again from Jesus to Peter)
	Yet thou art of his company.
	By thy face, well know I thee.
Peter	Woman, thou sayst amiss of me.
	I know the man no more than I know thee.

Woman   When they thy master in the garden took,
                 Then all thy fellows him forsook.
                 And now thou shouldst not him forsake.
                 For thou art of Galilee, I undertake.
Peter   I know him not, by God that made me.
                 You may believe me by this oath.
                 I take record before this company
                 That what I say to you is truth.

An actor within the pageant crows like a cock

Jesus looks up again towards Peter, who cannot meet his gaze

*The Woman looks from Jesus to Peter again, then to Caiphas and Annas, then
to the Knights. Defiantly she abases herself before Jesus, then goes on into the
pageant, L*

*Caiphas and Annas look suspicously at Peter, then come down the steps
towards the Knights and Jesus*

Caiphas   Lord Annas, what is your word?
                 This man deserves to be dead.
                 Yet if by the law alone we should be led,
                 He will clean escape.
Annas   Sir, it is my advice,
                 We should lead him to high justice
                 To Pilate that is wary and wise,
                 And has the law to keep.

*Caiphas nods. He gestures to 1st Knight, who pulls Jesus to his feet. Caiphas
and Annas go nearly to the top of the steps, one Knight following with Jesus.
They wait there*

2nd Knight goes on into the pageant

Peter advances to address the audience

Peter   Ah, well-a-day, well-a-day! False heart wilt thou not burst?
                 Since thy master so cowardly thou didst forsake!
                 Alas, where shall I now rest on the earth
                 Until he of his mercy to grace will me take?
                 I have forsaken my master and my Lord, Jesu,
                 Three times, as he told me I should do.
                 When I heard the cock crow, he cast on me a look,
                 As he would say, "Bethink thee what I said before."
                 Alas the time that ever I him forsook!
                 So shall I grieve from hence to evermore.

He goes into the pageant, L, as:

Pilate comes out of it, R, mounts the steps, and takes station on his rostrum

Caiphas and Annas bring Jesus before him

Caiphas	˙Sir Pilate, take heed to this thing.
	Jesus before you here we bring.
	From this city, unto the land of Galilee,
	He hath brought our laws into confusion,
	With his crafts, wrought by necromancy,
	Which he showeth to the people by false simulation.
Annas	Another crime, and worst of all,
	Against Caesar, our emperor, commits he.
	For "the King of the Jews" he himself doth call,
	So our great emperor's power of nought should be.
Pilate	Jesus, is this true what I hear, that thou art a king,
	And the son of God also,
	Lord of earth, and of everything?
	If this be true, then let me know.
Jesus	In Heaven is known my father's intent.
	Into this world I was born.
	By my father I was hither sent
	To seek for those that are forlorn.
	All that hear me, and in me believe,
	And keep faith with me steadfastly,
	Though they may die, I shall them revive,
	And bring them to enjoy bliss endlessly.
Pilate	Sirs, you have heard this man. How think ye?
	As he saith, it may well be.
	I find in him no objection
	Of treason. Nor no manner of guilt.
	The law will in no conclusion
	Without default allow his blood to be split.
Annas	Sir Pilate, the law resteth in thee.
	And we know truly his great trespass.
	To the emperor this matter told shall be
	If thou let Jesus from the judgement pass.
Pilate	Sirs, tell me one thing.
	What shall be his accusing?
Caiphas	Sir, we tell thee altogether,
	For his evil words we brought him hither.
	If he were not an evil-doer,
	We should not have brought him to you.
Pilate	Take him then, as you please.
	Deal with him as your law decrees.
Caiphas	It is not lawful for us, as is well known,
	That any manner of man should be slain.
	Therefore we bring this man to thee
	That said he would our king be.
	Well thou knowest, king we have none,
	But one emperor alone.
Pilate	Jesus, thou art king rightfully?
Jesus	So thou sayest to me.

Pilate	Tell me then, Where is thy kingdom?
Jesus	My kingdom is not in this world. So I tell thee in a word. If my kingdom here had been, Thus bound and delivered should I be seen?
Pilate	Sirs, advise you as ye can. I find no fault in this man.
Annas	There is a great record of mischief in this man. He hath converted many thousands since he began. He was born in the land of Galilee——
Pilate	Galilee? But you give me remission. If Jesus were born out of the land of Galilee. We have no power there, nor no jurisdiction. I understand right well what is to do. The judgement of Jesus lieth not on me. Herod Agrippa is king of that country, To judge it all its length and its breadth through. Therefore Jesus in haste to Herod lead, And commend me to King Herod with word and deed.

Caiphas and Annas exchange sour glances

| Annas | This errand sped shall be,
With all the haste that we can do.
We will tarry in no degree
Till Herod's presence we come to. |

They descend the steps with Jesus and the Knight, as:

Herod Agrippa, wearing a crown, comes out of the pageant, L

They meet him, C. Pilate remains where he is, pleased with himself. During the scene with Herod, spare members of the cast will begin to build up into an unidentified Crowd

Caiphas	Sir king, here Pilate hath sent A rascal to have judgement.
Herod	Welcome, Jesus, verament. I thank Pilate for this present. To send for thee has oft been my intent.
Caiphas	Most excellent king, you must take heed. He would destroy all this country, both old and young If he but ten months more proceed. By his preaching and false instruction, He leadeth the people into insurrection. And sayeth to all he is lord and the Jews' king.
Herod	Jesus, thou art welcome to me. I give Pilate great thanks for his sending. I have desired full long to see thee And of thy miracles to have knowing.

I have been told thou dost many a wondrous thing.
Thou makest the crooked straight, and the blind to see.
And to those that have been dead thou givest living.
And makest lepers fair and whole to be.
Now, Jesus, I pray thee, let me see.
A miracle in my presence.
Do it in haste now and with diligence
Since thy life and death lie here in me.

One of the crowd has been a one-armed Man—his other arm hidden under his polo-neck—who has come out of the pageant, L, with a Woman

Herod leads him to Jesus, so that Jesus can restore his arm. The man waves an empty sleeve in front of Jesus, who ignores him. Herod pushes the man back again

Jesus, why speakest thou not to thy king?
What is the cause thou standest here so still?
Thou knowest I may doom anything.
Thy life and death lie at my will.

He pulls Jesus to his feet, unbinds the rope, and throws it to the Knight

What? Thou unhanged harlot, why wilt thou not speak?
Hast thou scorn to speak unto thy king?
Because thou dost our laws break,
Do we affright you, then, with our talking?

Herod laughs. Crippled man joins in doltishly. Jesus stands mute

What! Speak, I say. Foul thing! Evil mayst thou fare.
The devil thy will shall break.
Sirs, beat his body with scourges bare,
And assay to make him speak.

Knight It shall be done without tarrying.
Come on, thou traitor, evil must thou be.
Why wilt thou not speak unto our king?
A new lesson we shall learn thee.

He rips off Jesus's polo-neck and throws it to the Woman. One of the crowd comes forward with an imaginary whip. The Knight lays it on Jesus's back. The crowd makes an "Ah" noise every time the "whip" strikes

Annas Jesus, thy bones we shall not break. (*Lash*)
But we shall make thee to skip. (*Lash*)
Thou hast lost thy tongue. (*Lash*) Thou dost not speak.
   (*Lash*)
How like you the voice of the whip? (*Lash*)

A Woman begins to laugh hysterically

Caiphas So spare not, sir, while thy strength doth last.
   (*Lash*)
Strike on. (*Lash*) He will speak in haste. (*Lash*)

Herod halts the scourging. The Woman's laugh cuts out

Herod
Cease, sirs. I command you. No more of this.
Jesus, thou thinkest this a good game.
For thou art strong to suffer shame,
And wouldst rather be beaten lame
Than all thy faults confess.
But I will not thy body spoil,
Nor put it here into more pain.
Sir, take Jesus at your own will
And lead him to Pilate back again.
Greet him well, and tell him certainly,
All my good friendship shall he have.
I give him power over Jesus. Then ye shall see
Whether he will this fellow doom or save.

Caiphas and Annas look at each other, and sign to the Knight. They lead Jesus back up the most convenient steps to Pilate. The crowd arrange themselves on both sets of steps to watch the trial

Herod goes into the pageant, L, to re-emerge as a member of the Crowd

Caiphas
Sir Pilate, good tindings hast thou now of me.
Of Herod the king thou hast good will.
And Jesus he sendeth again to thee.
And biddeth thee choose, him to save or spoil.

Annas
Yeay, sir, all the power lieth now in thee.
And thou knowest, against our faith he has been bent.
Thou knowest what mischief thereof may be.
We charge thee now to give judgement.

Pilate
Sirs, truly ye are to blame,
Jesus thus to beat, despoil and bind,
Or put him to so great shame.
For no fault in him I find.
Nor Herod neither to whom I sent you,
Fault in him could find right none,
But sent him to me again by you.
As ye know well, every one.
Therefore understand what I shall say.
You know the custom in this land,
Of your Pascal day which is near at hand.
What thief or traitor be in bond,
Without any price
To celebrate that day shall go free away.
Now I think that it were right
To let Jesus go as he might
And do him no more despite.
Sirs, that is my advice.
I would know what ye will say.

All (*shouting*) Nay! Nay! Nay!

Citizen	Deliver us the thief Barabbas
	That for murder condemned was.
Pilate	What shall I then with Jesus do,
	Whether he shall abide or go?
Another Citizen	Jesus shall on the cross be drawn.
	"Crucify!" we cry, each one.
All (*shouting*)	Crucify him!
Pilate	Sirs, what hath Jesus done amiss?
All (*shouting*)	Crucify him! Crucify him!
Pilate	Sirs, since you all would have it so,
	To put Jesus to woe and pain,
	Jesus awhile with me shall go.
	I shall examine him between us twain.

He signs to the Knight who releases Jesus's bound hands. Pilate takes Jesus over to the rostrum, L, opening an imaginary door to make an inner room of it

Jesus, what sayest thou, let me see.
This matter thou canst understand.
In peace thou might be for all of me,
But for the people of thy land.
Bishops and priests of the law,
They love thee not as thou mayst see,
And the common people against thee draw.
In peace thou might be aye for me.
This I tell thee plain.

Jesus stands silent

What sayest thou, Jesus? Speak between us two.
Thou knowest I have power on the cross to doom thee.
And also I have power to let thee go.
What canst thou say unto me?

Jesus	Over me thou hast no power
	But what my father hath granted before.
	I come my father's will to fulfil
	That mankind may not come to ill.
	He that hath betrayed me at this time,
	His trespass is more than mine.

Caiphas speaks to the people

Caiphas	Ye princes and masters, take heed and see
	How Pilate is biased towards this fellow favourably.
	Thus all our laws destroyed may be.

Pilate leaves Jesus

Pilate	Sirs, what will ye now with Jesus do?
	I can find in him naught but good.
	It is in my conscience you should let him go.

	It were regret to spill his blood.
Annas	If thou let Jesus from us pass.
	This word I swear we shall uphold.
	Thou shalt answer for this trespass,
	And traitor to the emperor be called.

The crowd growls its agreement

Pilate   Now since ye will no other way,
                    But only that Jesus must die,
                    Bring me some water, I pray thee.

A Servant—from the crowd—brings him an imaginary basin of water

                    And what I will do, you shall see.
                    I wash with water my hands clean.
                    So guiltless of his death I be.
Citizen   Let his blood lie on us.
2nd Citizen   And our children after us.
Crowd   Yeah! Yeah!

Pilate goes to the rostrum, L, and brings Jesus to them

Pilate   Lo, sirs, I bring him here to your presence
                    That ye may know I find in him no offence.
Citizen   Deliver him. And let us go.
                    On the cross he shall mop and mow.

Laughter from the crowd

Pilate   Shall I nail to the cross your king in all his power?
Citizen   We have no king but the emperor.
Pilate   Since every way it must be so,
                    Then we must our office do.
                    Bring forth to the bar those who must be doomed
                    And we shall give judgement in this room.

The Knight arbitrarily calls someone from the crowd to be Barabbas

                    Barabbas, hold up thy hand,
                    Here at the judgement thou dost stand.
                    Sirs, what say ye of Barabbas, traitor and thief?
                    Shall he go free, or shall he die the death?
Crowd   Free! Free!
Caiphas   Sir, for the solemnity of our Pascal day,
                    He shall go free away.
Pilate   Barabbas, here I dismiss thee.
                    And give thee licence to go free.

Barabbas joyfully rejoins his mates. The crowd cry "Barabbas! Barabbas!"

                    Jesus, thine own people have disproved
                    All that I have for thee said or moved.
                    Therefore (*to the Crowd*)

First you shall the clothes from Jesus tear,
And make him naked for to be.
With whips you shall scourge him on his body bare.
So that all men may see.
When he is beaten, crown him for your king.
Then to the cross, you shall him bring.
(*To Jesus*)
Upon the cross, they shall fasten thee.
Three nails into thy body will driven be.
One shall through thy right hand go,
Another through thy left hand also.
The third shall smite through both thy feet.
Yet thou shalt not hang alone,
But either side there shall hang down
Thieves one and two along with thee,
Upon the mount of Calvary.

Pilate walks scornfully down the steps, R, *those members of the crowd who have been cluttering it up, falling away in a tumble to leave it free. Caiphas and Annas, wary, follow him down, and into the pageant,* R

Knight brings Jesus down the steps. Two women from the crowd have gone back into the pageant, but what others remain are now on either side of the lower area with Jesus in a cleared space in the middle. A pause. They move slowly in towards him, then rush at him, bear him down, hit and tear. They strip off his (weakened) trousers and shoes, leaving him with only a loincloth

A Woman goes into the pageant, gets a crown of thorns, and crowns him

Knight   Now be thou gladly our king.

Two men lift Jesus on their shoulders, and take him in a circle, presenting him to the audience. The crowd ad lib. "Hail, king!" "Roll up for the king!" etc., dancing before and behind. Jesus completes the circle, and is then toppled on to the ground

The two women of Jerusalem who vanished earlier have now reappeared to watch, but as new (and horrified) characters

Knight (*with an obeisance as Jesus topples*) Here thy reign is beginning.
1st Woman Alas, Jesus! Alas! Woe is me
               That thou art thus despoiled, alas!
               Never yet was fault found in thee.
               Ever thou hast been full of grace.
2nd Woman Here is a rueful sight of Jesus so good,
               That he should die against all right.
               Ah, wicked men, be ye more than wood
               To do this good lord such a great despite.
Jesus   Daughters of Jerusalem, for me weep not.
               But for yourselves weep, and for your children also.
               For the day shall come that this day's work hath wrought,

When this sin and blindness shall turn all to woe.
Then shall be said, "Blessed be the wombs that barren be,
And woe to the breasts on which the babies be suckling."
To their fathers they shall say, "Woe to that day thou didst
    beget me."
And to their mothers, "Alas, where be our dwelling?"
Then to the hills and mountains, they shall cry and call,
"Rise up and hide us from the face of him sitting in throne.
Or else erupt and on us come and fall,
That we may be hid and freed from our sorrow and pain."

Most of the crowd back away, abashed, into the pageant. The Women go

The Knight and an Assistant are left with Jesus. The Knight indicates that he should lift the cross. It is too heavy

Simon of Cyrene comes out of the pageant, R, *followed by a man*

Knight   He seemeth weary of his way.
                Some help to get, I will assay.
                (*To Simon*)
                Sir, to thee a word of good,
                A man is here, as thou may see,
                Who bears a burden made of wood.
                Whereon he shall hanged be.
                Therefore this I pray of thee.
                Take thou the cross from the man.
                Bear it with us to Calvary.
                And great thanks shalt thou earn.

Simon   Sirs, I may not in no degree.
                I have great errands for to do.
                Therefore I pray ye, excuse me,
                And about my business let me go.

Knight   What, harlot, hast thou scorn
                To bear the tree when I pray it?
                Thou shalt bear it, errands or none,
                Were it ten times the weight.

Simon   Sirs, I pray you, displease thee nought.
                I will help to bear the tree.
                Into that place it shall be brought
                Wherever thou wilt command me.

Hastily Simon helps Jesus with the cross, and together they carry it up the steps, R. *The Man follows. They lay it on top of the pageant by the rostrum,* L

One of the Women, who is old, and wears a headscarf, has come up the steps, L

Woman   Ah, sinful people, why fare ye thus?
                For sweat and blood, he may not see.
                Alas, holy prophet, Christ Jesus.
                (*She wipes his face with her kerchief*)

My heart is full of care for thee.
Jesus   Veronica, thy wiping doth me ease.
My face is clean, that was black to see.
I shall keep them from all misease
That look on thy kerchief, and remember me.

Knight motions Woman out of the way, and she clears upstage C

Knight   Come on now. Here we shall assay
Whether he and the cross will suit.
Cast him down now here in the devil's way.
How long shall he be standing on his feet?

The cross is T-shaped and ten feet high. Into the centre of the rostrum, L, has been built a box into which the bottom of the cross will fit tightly. This box has been bolted to the framework of the pageant. The bottom two feet of the cross will fit exactly into it. One foot above the top of the rostrum there is a small platform on which Jesus will stand, and to which his feet will (theoretically) be nailed. There are handholds on the arms of the cross, painted the same colour as the cross itself, and holes for the nails to fit. Upstage, behind the pageant, suspended from the flies, there hangs a rope, ending in a hook. While the Assistant lifts the T of the cross, the Knight attaches this hook into a ring set in the back of the T. Consequently, when the cross is raised, it has support at top and bottom, and stagehands in the flies will assist it by pulling on the rope and tying off. When the cross is in position, a wire at the back of the pageant is attached to another bolt at the back of the cross at the middle, so that it is further braced

Now give me his arm in haste.
His good days now be past.

Jesus lies on the cross

Fast on the rope, and pull it long.
And I will draw on again.
Spare we not these ropes strong,
Though we bruise both flesh and vein.

A stout leather belt with a buckle has been fastened to the centre of the cross. Assistant has unfastened the buckle while Knight has been getting the rope. Now he buckles the belt round Jesus's waist, during the lines that refer to "rope". The Assistant will be a double for Herod Agrippa, and during his last trip into the pageant he has picked up his mallet and nails

Now drive in a nail, and let us see
How well the flesh and sinews last.

Assistant drives a nail as if into one hand. Jesus gives a cry

Assistant There I grant, and so shouldst thee,
That nail is smitten well and fast.
Knight   Now let me drive in
This little iron pin.

The second nail goes in. Not so loud a cry

That, I dare say, will last.
As ever I hope to win,
His arm is but a fin.
Drive thou the last one in.

Assistant puts a nail between the legs. A moan. Knight ties the legs

And now we draw him fast.

Pilate comes out of the pageant, L, *and up the steps, followed by Caiphas and Annas. Pilate has a paper on which is written "JESUS OF NAZARETH— THE KING OF THE JEWS". The paper has a strip of Velcro at the top, so that it can easily be fastened to the platform on which Jesus stands*

Pilate   Come hither, thou! I command thee.

Knight approaches

Hang this paper to the tree.
Since he the King of Jews will be,
He must have cognizance.
"Jesus of Nazareth" men may see,
"King of the Jews". How like it ye?
I wrote it there, since so said he,
With no variance.

Knight attaches the paper to the platform

Caiphas   Sir Pilate, we are amazed at this,
                    That thou shouldst write him to be King of Jews.
Annas   Rather it were thou shouldst write thus,
                    That he *called* himself King of Jews.
Pilate   What I have written is written.

He and Caiphas and Annas retire to the rostrum, R, *to watch*

A crowd has gathered on the steps, the Man at the top of the steps, R *Mary comes out of the pageant,* R, *and Magdalene,* L. *Both remain at the bottom of their respective steps*

1st Citizen   Look! Here's a fellow lying on a tree.
2nd Citizen   Yeay! And I'm sure he is a worthy king.
3rd Citizen   Sir, tell me now what help is thy prophecy.
4th Citizen   Or any of thy false preaching.
1st Citizen   Sirs, set up the cross on high,
                    That we may look him in the face.
2nd Citizen   So shall we kneel our king to magnify,
                    And pray him of his grace.

The cross is set up on the rostrum, Simon and the Man helping the Knight and his Assistant

1st Citizen   Hail, King of the Jews! If thou be he.

2nd Citizen	Sir, thou hang'st like flesh and bones.
3rd Citizen	Come down now off that tree.
4th Citizen	And join us in our revelry.

The Crowd laugh

1st Citizen   Now if thou canst do such a deed
Help thyself as best thou can.
And we will believe thee without dread,
And say thou art a mighty man.

General laughter

Jesus   Oh Father Almighty, maker of man,
Forgive these Jews that do me woe.
Forgive them, Father forgive them pain.
For they know not what they do.

Caiphas   Lo, sirs, behold and see.
Here hangeth he that helped many a man.
Now, if God's son he be,
Let him help himself if he can.

Annas   If thou king of Israel be,
Come down from the cross among us all.
Let thy god deliver thee,
And then our king we will thee call.

Jesus   Eloi, eloi, lama sabathana!
My God, my God, I speak to thee,
Why hast thou forsaken me?

Knight   How! Hear ye not, as well as I,
How he can now on "holy" cry?

Assistant   There is none holy in this country
To deliver him from this quandary.

Jesus   My thirst is sore; my thirst is sore.

Knight   Thou shalt have a drink therefore.

A pole with a sponge on it is passed up from the pageant by the crowd on the steps, L. Knight offers it

Your thirst, Sir Yobbo, for to slake,
Vinegar and gall here I take.
Is not this a good drink?

Jesus's head lolls away from it

To cry for drink thou hadst great haste.
Now me seems it is but a waste.

Knight gives the pole to one of the crowd

Jesus   Now is my passion brought to an end.
Father in heaven, into thy hand
I commend my soul.

*An ASM at the side of the pageant, R, shakes a thunder-sheet which is hanging
in view of the audience. Lighting change: the stage is darkened with the cross,
Mary and Magdalene lighted*

Pilate leaves quickly. Assistant, Knight and some of the crowd scurry away

*A moment. Simon of Cyrene goes over to the cross, rips off the notice and
hands it to Caiphas. Then he walks down the steps, R, and into the pageant,
followed by the two bishops*

*A moment. The picture is of Mary and Magdalene each at the bottom of steps,
the Old Woman upstage C, Jesus on the cross*

Mary   Alas, my son, my life, my dear.
                    Look on thy mother, that thee bore.
                    Thou wast my child. I fostered thee.
                    I gave thee suck upon my knee.
                    Upon my pain have thou pity.

Magdalene (*beginning to climb the steps*) Alas! How stand I on my feet
                    When I think on his wounds that bleed?
                    Jesus, that was loving and sweet,
                    And never did ill.
                    Now dead. And to be buried in mud and grit
                    Without skill.

Woman   Without skill these Jews each one,
                    Our lovely Lord they have him slain,
                    And trespass did he never none
                    On any head.
                    To whom now shall we make our moan?
                    Our Lord is dead.

Mary (*mounting the steps*) Alas! Now is my life forlorn,
                    To find my son tugged, lugged, all torn
                    With traitors on this tide,
                    With nails thrust, and crown of thorn,
                    So I shall cry, both even and morn,
                    That my boy that I have born,
                    With bitter death must bide.

Magdalene (*kneeling at the cross downstage*) Alas! How should my heart be
                         light
                    To see my seemly Lord in sight
                    Dolefully drawn and torn in spite
                    That never did man grievance.
                    May God that ever rules the right
                    Give to the men who failed to fight
                    For Jesus, much mischance.

Woman (*kneeling at the foot of the cross*) Alas! Sorrow sets me sore.
                    Mirth of thee, Lord, I have no more.
                    Why wouldst thou die, Jesus? Wherefore?
                    That to the dead gave life.
                    Help me, Jesus, with some thing.

	Me from this bitter sorrow may thou bring,
	Or else slay me, or anything
	To stint my soul of strife.
Magdalene	Come down, Lord, and break thy bands.
	Loose and heal thy lovely hands,
	Since thou art god and man.
	I see thee, Lord, in such unpeace,
	My grief will not slake or cease,
	Such sorrow is me upon.

Peter leaves the pageant, L and comes up the steps. While

Mary	Alas, alas! I live too long
	To see my sweet son with pains strong,
	Like a thief on the cross hung.
	My sweet son to death is dressed.
	Now is my care too much increased.
	And my heart with pain is pressed.
Peter (*crossing to her*)	Blessed Mary, change thy thought,
	For though thy son with sorrow be sought,
	By his own will this work was wrought.
	To keep you all he charged me here.
	I am your servant, my lady dear.
	Wherefore I pray you, be of good cheer.
Mary	Would he had never of me been born.
	I see his flesh all torn,
	On back behind, on breast before,
	Rent with wounds wide.
Magdalene	Needs must we dwell in woe
	To see our friend with many a foe,
	All rent from top to toe,
	So to abide.
Peter	Blessed ladies, take heed to what I tell.
	Had he not died, we should to Hell,
	Among fields evermore to dwell,
	And in pain to smart.
	He suffered death for our trespass,
	And through his death we shall have grace,
	To dwell with him and find in Heaven a place.
	Therefore be merry in heart.
Mary	Dear friend, well know I this,
	That he doth buy us to his bliss.
	Yet let me kiss before I go
	His blessed feet that suffered woe,
	Nailed on this tree.
	Then will I come with thee,
	No longer this sight to see.
	And thou mayst guide us as it pleaseth thee.
Peter	All your desire shall be wrought.

> With hearty will, shall I work your thought.
> But, blessed Mary, tarry not.
> In the temple best ye were.
> (*He helps the Old Woman up*)
> For holy prayer may change your mood,
> And cause your cheer to be more good.

Old Woman and Magdalene go down the steps, L

> When you see not your child's blood,
> The less may be your care.

Uneasily, he follows the two women down the steps, L. *The Lights fade, so that only the cross is lit. Mary comes from her place at the top of the steps,* R, *to the cross. She kneels and clasps Jesus's feet. She begins to moan. The Lights fade*

THE END OF THE PLAY

All Lights up for the curtain. Let the other actors help Jesus off the cross before coming forward for applause. They should return to the pageant and wait while the auditorium empties

FURNITURE AND PROPERTY LIST

ACT I

On stage: Tree of knowledge with apples
Stools for actors
2 full-length mirrors

All props, used as follows:
Mitre, crook **(God)**
Cloak **(Gabriel)**
Cloak **(Angel)**
Black half-mask with curving horns **(Satan)**
2 fig leaves **(Tree)**
Toy lamb **(Abel)**
Sack of sheaves **(Cain)**
Blood capsule **(Cain)**
Pillow strapped to belly **(Elizabeth)**
Pillow, cord **(Actor)**
False white beard **(Joseph)**
Fez or turban with crown **(1st King)**
Fez or turban with crown **(2nd King)**
Fez or turban with crown **(3rd King)**
Elaborate crown **(Herod)**
Sheepskin, pipe/whistle, handkerchief **(3rd Shepherd)**
Sheepskin, mittens, handkerchief **(1st Shepherd)**
Sheepskin, handkerchief, hat **(2nd Shepherd)**
Ragged cloak **(Mak)**
2 sacks, headscarf **(Gil)**
Gold **(1st King)**
Incense **(2nd King)**
Myrrh **(3rd King)**
Wooden swords **(1st** and **2nd Knights)**
Pillows **(1st, 2nd, 3rd Women)**

ACT II

Strike: Tree of knowledge
All Act I props

Set: Large cross with leather belt on it

Props, used as follows:
Mask **(Satan)**
Vial **(Magdalene)**
Haloes **(John, Peter, James, Philip)**
Water jar **(Man)**

Toga **(Pilate)**
Wooden swords **(1st and 2nd Knights** at Pilate's court)
Gown **(Doctor)**
Cardinal's hat, money bag **(Caiphas)**
Cardinal's hat **(Annas)**
Long apron **(Porter)**
Sword **(Peter)**
Rope **(Doctor)**
Crown **(Herod Agrippa)**
Crown of thorns **(Woman)**
Headscarf **(Woman)**
Mallet, nails **(Assistant)**
Paper with "Jesus of Nazareth—the King of the Jews" **(Pilate)**
Pole with sponge **(Crowd member)**
Thunder-sheet **(ASM)**

LIGHTING PLOT

Property fittings required: nil

An open stage

ACT I

To open: House lights up

Cue 1	When actors are seated and have checked their props *House lights down, lighting on pageant area*	(Page 1)
Cue 2	As Adam and Eve descend to ground area *Lighting on ground area*	(Page 7)
Cue 3	**Cain** turns back to **Abel**'s body, with blood dripping from his mouth *Fade lighting on pageant*	(Page 14)
Cue 4	**Satan** crawls on his belly towards **Cain** *Fade all lighting except area round body*	(Page 14)
Cue 5	**Satan** stands, resting ǫn **Cain**'s head or shoulder, while **Cain** lours brutishly at audience *Fade to black-out*	(Page 14)
Cue 6	Two **Angels** enter *Lighting on top of pageant*	(Page 14)
Cue 7	**Gabriel** advances to meet **Mary** *Lighting on lower area*	(Page 14)
Cue 8	**Elizabeth** walks round front of pageant *Lighting on ground area*	(Page 15)
Cue 9	**Gabriel** goes on into the pageant *Fade lights; then bring up lighting*	(Page 21)
Cue 10	**Herod** comes down steps R *Fade lights on pageant and on all but area already used for* **Cain** *and* **Satan**	(Page 46)
Cue 11	**Herod** screams and raves, out of control *Fade to black-out*	(Page 46)
Cue 12	As vendors shout their wares *Snap up full stage and auditorium lighting*	(Page 47)

ACT II

To open: Full general lighting

Cue 13	As ASM shakes thunder-sheet *Fade to lighting on cross,* **Mary** *and* **Magdalene**	(Page 74)

Cue 14   **Peter** follows the two women down the steps, L   (Page 76)
          Fade to lighting on cross only

Cue 15   **Mary** kneels and clasps **Jesus**'s feet, moaning   (Page 76)
          Fade to black-out

MADE AND PRINTED IN GREAT BRITAIN BY
LATIMER TREND & COMPANY LTD PLYMOUTH

MADE IN ENGLAND